D1636524

WHO AM I AFTER SPORTS?

An Athlete's Roadmap to Discover
New Purpose and Live Fulfilled

DARRYLL STINSON

Printed in the United States of America

Published by Author Academy Elite
PO Box 43, Powell, OH 43065
www.AuthorAcademyElite.com

Identifiers:
LCCN: 2020916807
ISBN: 978-1-64746-480-6 (paperback)
ISBN: 978-1-64746-481-3 (hardback)

Available in paperback, hardback, e-book, and audiobook

Any Internet addresses (websites, blogs, etc.) and telephone
numbers printed in this book are offered as a resource. They are
not intended in any way to be or imply an endorsement by Second
Chance Athletes, nor does Second Chance Athletes vouch for the
content of these sites and numbers for the life of this book.

All Scripture quotations, unless otherwise indicated, are taken
from the Holy Bible, New International Version®, NIV®.
Copyright © 1973, 1978, 1984 by Biblica, Inc.™ Used by
permission of Zondervan. All rights reserved worldwide.

Some names and identifying details have been changed to
protect the privacy of individuals.

Book design by Jetlaunch. Cover design by Melt Project.

Dedication to a Real One
I dedicate this book to the late Elder Mike White and Francis White.

Elder Mike, without your heart and commitment to serve others and keep athletes focused on the greatest purpose in life, I wouldn't be where I am or who I am today. You built the bridge I traveled on from suicide to success and significance. You taught me "I'm here to serve" is one of the most powerful sentences a man can say. You always believed in me, and you knew the impact this book and my story would have on the world.

Thank you. I love and miss you dearly.

Ms. Francis, I love you. There would be no Darryll Stinson if there were no Francis White keeping Mike White together. You were the wind beneath his wings, and your impact on his life and mind will always be appreciated.

My only regret in writing this book was that I allowed my fear and insecurities to prevent me from finishing it sooner, so you and Elder Mike could enjoy reading it together. The good news, as I alluded to in my words to Elder Mike, is that he already saw this day in his mind. I'll never forget how excited he got when I shared with him the vision for the book and Second Chance Athletes.

He said, "Ahhhhh ... my boy D! Pretty soon Bishop T.D. Jakes is going to be interviewing you for advice!" It had absolutely nothing to do with the book, and he said all that and more before I finished sharing my vision with him. Lol. #classiceldermike

---

Badge 1457

ACKNOWLEDGEMENTS

To my wife, Brittany
You're amazing. You listened as I brainstormed, wrote, doubted, quit, restarted, complained, yelled and completed this book. You mothered our children while I wrote early mornings and late nights. You put your dreams on hold so I could pursue mine. You were my refuge, my editor, my assistant, my lover and friend I needed to complete this project. Thank you. Our best days are ahead.

To my daughters
You're my joy—the smiles I look forward to seeing when I get home and my motivation to reach my fullest potential. You're smart, beautiful and have the best senses of humor. I love you. You'll always be daddy's babies. #girldad

To my family
Mom (Yolanda), dad (Darrel), Stacey (stepmom), Greta (aka 'Grandmutha'). You've invested in me in ways I can never repay. From driving hours to support me in a game that I never got playing time, to cheering for me when I was receiving national attention, you were always there for me.

To my siblings
Chas, Nacole, Ashlee, Bri (basically), Baby D, and Taylor. I love y'all. We're all going to do great things.

To all my aunts, uncles, cousins, in-laws, elders, grandparents, church family, and sons and daughters in the faith.
I wouldn't be the man I am without you. I wouldn't have made it through hard seasons of life without your continuous support. I love you and am honored to share this journey.

To my fans and supporters.
You're the wind beneath my wings. I'm extremely humbled that you place your faith in me and whatever dream I'm building. Thank you for your continued support.

To Pastors Travis and Tina
You believed in me when I struggled to believe in myself. You called out the greatness that was inside of me. You prayed me, my wife and our family THROUGH. We love you guys. This you know.

Lastly ...

Thank you to everyone who called, texted, prayed, donated, commented on social media, read an article I was featured in or cheered me on from the stands. No act of kindness was too small. Each one made a positive impact on my life. And I want you to know how much I love and appreciate you.

Thank you!
Darryll Stinson

MAJOR DISCLAIMERS—
PLEASE GIVE ME GRACE

**1. I don't think athletes are the most superior
beings on the planet.**
My wife and three editors all voiced concern about the
tone of my writing at times throughout this book. My
gratitude for the work ethic athletics can develop within
athletes at times may sound as if I believe athletes are
superior to others. I don't believe that. It was too challenging to extract that from the writing without losing
my natural voice. So, I made an executive decision to
leave those places as my authentic writing voice and
clarify my heart and beliefs in this section.

- I don't think athletes are superior to others.
- I believe sports are a great tool to develop persistence, grit, tenacity, mental toughness, leader-

ship, teamwork and other valuable transferable skillsets.

* I neither think athletes are the only high achievers on the planet, nor do I believe athletes have a special gift from God to be more tenacious. I believe the mindset and skillset many athletes possess due to their involvement in sports also can be cultivated by other industries and experiences. Consider it your Secret Sauce Skills. I believe being pushed to the max physically and mentally in high-pressure environments, with hundreds or thousands of fans watching, develops men and women in a way other forms of development do not. I believe this development gives athletes who have embraced the process described in this book—I call it The Athlete Transition Roadmap—an edge among people who don't have similar experiences.

Please don't attack me for my beliefs. If you're not an athlete and you're reading this, I believe in you and know that you have gifts and talents that will make an impact in this world.

2. Don't get confused by timelines.

At times, it may seem like I was in college, then three years out of college, then somehow back in college again. The reason why is that I wanted you to know how "up and down" and "back and forth" transitioning can be. There were times where I thought I couldn't care less about being an athlete, and the desire to compete as an athlete was long gone. Then a few months or years later, those feelings or hunger to be an athlete again would consume my mind like a flood. Sometimes I resisted the urge to entertain those thoughts. Other times, I let it push me back into a three-day depression.

The Athlete Transition Roadmap, although outlined in phases/steps, was not linear. Maybe with this book your process will be, but if not, no worries—you're not alone.

3. The Athlete Transition Roadmap can be applied to anyone in transition.

This book was written for athletes, but the principles are transferable to any identity and career transitions. I've been told by CEOs, military veterans, and people who have been through divorces that this process was helpful in their transitions.

Keep that in mind and share The Athlete Transition Roadmap with anyone who needs a plan to help them through life's challenging transitions.

4. I am not a therapist, and mental illness is real.

This book will help you live a more mentally healthy life, but if you're battling depression, anxiety or other mental illnesses, please see a professional counselor or therapist. I, Darryll Stinson, the mental health coach, still see a counselor. I advise you to see one as well.

5. My family's impact in my life is immeasurable.

I chose to dedicate this book to the late Elder Mike White because of his impact on my life in relation to the content of this book and the tragedy of his passing. However, I owe every day of my life to my family. I have been beyond blessed with a supportive family. From birth, my mom, dad, step parents, cousins, uncles, aunts, sisters and grandparents have been there for me when I was on the front page of the newspaper for my athletic success and when I was "riding the bench" during a summer basketball game that they drove two hours away to see me play. And now I have my wife, Brittany, and my amazing daughters, Ava, Arianna and Amaya. Plus, my family-in-law, church family, fans and supporters. I have so much to be grateful for.

Thank you to everyone who called, texted, prayed, donated, commented on social media, read an article I was featured in or cheered from the stands. No act of kindness was too small. Each made a positive impact on my life. And I want you to know how much I love and appreciate you.

FOREWORD

At seven years old, I was like many young boys: all sports all the time. My heroes were professional athletes. Nearly every game I played was related to sports. The only part of the newspaper I read was the sports page. My aunt, who was a lawyer, once asked me what I wanted to be when I grew up.

"A football player," I said.

She laughed. "OK, Chris, if you can't play football, what do you want to be when you grow up?"

"A basketball player."

A bit frustrated, she sighed, yet kept trying. "If you don't make it as a football or a basketball player, what do you want to be?"

"A baseball player."

That type of thinking can have tragic consequences. If you don't make it to pros, then what? Or even if you do play at the highest level, what happens when your career is over? Too often the answer is that you lose your sense of self. With your identity wrapped up in your athletic ability, your last game can lead to days, months, even years of misery.

But it doesn't have to be that way. No matter how great you are in sports, your identity should not be rooted in how well you dribble a basketball, catch a football, or hit a baseball.

But how do you get to that healthy place, that place where you feel good about yourself even when the cheering stops, even when there are no more games to be played?

One way to get there is to read this book. Darryll Stinson has seen this issue from both sides. He's been the guy who was football or bust and, thankfully, he's become the man who is now comfortable—and happy and fulfilled—in his own skin, even when the gridiron is no longer a part of his life.

As a sports reporter for more than three decades, I've seen many struggle with the question of, "Who am I beyond an athlete?" That question can gnaw at you at the end of your career or even at the height of your success. Either way, it brings weariness and distress. It's no way to live.

Darryll is as qualified as anyone to address this topic. His story is raw and transparent. Baring his soul, he reveals the pain and self-destructive behavior that not knowing your true identity can bring. His journey was not without scars, but that is a good thing. Because those scars have stories.

Stories of healing. Stories of redemption. Stories of triumph. Stories that can lead you to discover who you are after sports.

Chris Broussard
FOX Sports broadcaster and NBA analyst
Founder and president of The K.I.N.G. Movement

ENDORSEMENTS

"I believe Darryll's work is vital to the success and wellness of athletes in transition across the globe. If you've ever asked yourself the question "What's next after sports?" this book will help you find and build the next season of your life."

—Jack Canfield, bestselling author of the Chicken Soup for the Soul Series, The Success Principles and featured teacher in "The Secret"

"The Wuerffel Trophy signifies service, impact, and inspiration—all three things that Darryll walks out in his life every day. This book is a snapshot of how Darryll made it from suicide to success and how you can see the same success in your life. I believe what Darryll says, 'Your best days are still ahead of you.'"

—Danny Wuerffel, 1996 Heisman Trophy winner and executive director of Desire Street Ministries

"Inspiring … actionable … and transformative. Darryll shares a transition framework that not only helps athletes but anyone in a season of finding a new identity and path in life."

—Buddy Curry, former Atlanta Falcons player and founder of Kids & Pros

"With clear, concise, and inspiring content, Darryll offers a roadmap that guides athletes through depression after sports to create their dream life. If you're one of the many athletes who struggle with transition, this book is the perfect place to start making changes."

—Brian Pruitt, First Team Associated Press All American running back and Founder/CEO of Power of Dad

"Transition can be a scary word for athletes, but Who Am I After Sports? helps give them the confidence to excel after their athletic career ends."

—David Meltzer, co-founder of Sports 1 Marketing, best-selling author and top business coach

"Having worked with thousands of elite athletes and high-performers, I know this book is going to equip athletes with the necessary framework to overcome after-sports depression and move toward the life of their dreams."

—Grant Parr, mental performance coach, author, and 90% Mental podcast host

CONTENTS

CHAPTER 1

WILL THERE EVER BE ANYTHING LIKE SPORTS?

Let's get this out of the way.

There is nothing like sports.

There is nothing like pushing yourself physically to the max day after day and week after week. There's no feeling quite like the adrenaline rush you get when competition is fierce, and the stakes are high. There are few things in life that bring the joy, excitement and energy that winning a championship does. There is nothing like making a game-winning play and hearing the electric thunder from hundreds, thousands and millions of people cheering for you and your team. Nothing stimulates your ego like people asking for your autograph, media lining up to interview you, and having the world's attention centered on you.

The reality is that nothing can or will ever be just like sports.

This presents major challenges for athletes who face the end of their career.

Just consider the statistics:

- Fewer than 1 percent of high school athletes will play college athletics.[1]
- Fewer than 4 percent of college athletes will play professionally.[2]
- College students who were highly invested in their athletic selves reported experiencing a keen sense of loss in their overall identities when transitioning out of intercollegiate athletics. They reported feeling lost, confused and void of life.[3]
- One study conducted by the Washington University School of Medicine in St. Louis found that 52 percent of retired NFL players reported using prescription painkillers during their careers, and 71 percent of that group met the criteria for misuse.[4]
- College athletes whose careers ended unexpectedly experienced difficult transitions as they felt "cheated out of four years."[5]
- 78 percent of all NFL players are divorced, bankrupt or unemployed two years after leaving the game.[6]
- Exceptional demands of high-level sport can prevent athletes from engaging in a wide range of developmental tasks across their lifespan, including those that are needed to form a mature and well-rounded identity.[7]

That's the sad reality. The good news for you and every other athlete who will face the end of an athletic career is that you have the power to find something more fulfilling than sports. Now before you roll your eyes or internally dismiss what I just said, I'll give you the main theme of this entire book to prove my point. In chapters three through seven, I'll guide you through a five-step process I call the Athlete Transition Roadmap. In short, the roadmap covers: (1) How to accept the end of your athletic career; (2) Why you should believe in a greater future; (3) How to discover your purpose; (4) Why you are wired to pursue your dreams like a champion; (5) Your persistence will allow you to become a renewed, elite individual.

I found a life more fulfilling than sports. If I found it, so will you. I know that's a bold promise, but here's what I believe. Regardless of what caused you to stop playing—an injury, not having the right opportunity, a bad coach, a lack of money, politics, a bad decision, you name it—the rest of your life can still be the best of your life. I won't argue with you about whether or not you were meant to play sports—you obviously were. We all play sports for some of our lives, but none of us can play high-level sports for ALL of our lives. Every athlete in the world faces the time when he must hang up the cleats, fold away the jersey, shoot her last shot or cross his last finish line. It's inevitable. That means all athletes must, at some point, find their identities outside of their roles as athletes and find a purpose beyond sports. That's what this book is all about. Finding your identity, discovering your purpose, and living fulfilled in your life beyond sports.

As a result of the end of your career, you may struggle with questions such as:

- Who am I?
- Why do I feel this way?

- How do I "get over" sports?
- Will my life ever be fun and exciting again?
- What am I supposed to do with my life now that my career is finished?
- Will I ever be great at anything like I was at sports?

A lack of answers to those questions made me feel like I had embraced, and forever lost, my one true purpose.

A lack of answers to those questions drove me to the darkest depression of my life.

A lack of answers to those questions made me suicidal. Fortunately, I lived to share my story.

I wrote this book to help you find answers I couldn't when my athletic career was finished. My prayer is that these pages won't just help you feel better but will equip you to live better—in all areas of your life. I want you to have massive clarity of your purpose and identity. I want you to fulfill dreams above your wildest imagination and impact the lives of others for generations to come. And I want you to do all of this while appreciating the gift that athletics was to you as well as healing the wounds you incurred along your journey.

Welcome to life after sports. Where your best days are ahead.

CHAPTER 2
WHAT HAPPENED?

It was Friday, August 17, 2012. I, a 6'5" former Division I athlete, lay shivering violently on a freezing metal hospital bed in the psychiatric unit at Henry Ford Hospital in Detroit, Michigan.

A broad-shouldered, middle-aged doctor walked into my room, introduced himself, and said, "So, tell me, Darryll ... why did you attempt to kill yourself?" He asked in a way that I could tell he was used to seeing people at their worst.

"Leave me alone! I just want to die!" I responded, holding my pumping stomach and clenching my teary-wet eyes.

The pain of trying to answer that question was unbearable.

I couldn't think clearly. Thoughts were racing through my mind like a NASCAR speedway. I spent the previous few weeks overdosing on painkillers, smoking ounces of marijuana, trying to starve myself to death, and drinking to the point of blackout. In just a few weeks, my 275-pound muscular build had been reduced to a 219-pound, frail-looking skeleton.

My mother, father and a few other family members were with me. My grandmother was speeding to the hospital from our hometown, Jackson. Everyone was asking themselves the same two questions.

How in the world did Darryll get to this point? And, what did we do wrong?

For as long as I could remember, I had been motivated, driven, productive, and a source of encouragement to others. I earned good grades. I had a phenomenal work ethic. I was popular and charismatic. I excelled at multiple sports. I was voted most likely to succeed by my classmates in high school. I loved to volunteer and help others. I had a huge support system of friends, family and fans that loved and adored me. From the outside looking in, I had nothing to be depressed about and everything to be grateful for.

What changed? **How did I go from living the "good life" to wanting to end my life?**

I'll tell you how.

My athletic career ended.

The very thing that I had worked my entire life to achieve was stripped away due to a back injury.

One reason why my athletic career ending was so traumatic was that sports had become my identity from an early age.

As a child, I always wanted to be … a super star… a global influencer. I thought I would achieve fame by rapping, writing best-selling fiction books and directing Oscar-nominated movies. Who knows? Maybe that will still happen.

I was a smart kid and excelled in school. My mother wisely placed me in accelerated learning classes in the third grade so I could challenge myself. It made me one of two black kids in my entire class, yet I was OK with that because no one hassled me. My peers thought I was cool, and since I was so smart, a lot of them asked for my help with homework or just borrowed my homework so they could copy it.

I was confident, outgoing and probably had a pretty big ego.

Everything changed when I overheard a group of black students laughing as I walked past them in the hallway. Being the extravert that I was, I walked over to them and asked,

"Hey ya'll, what's so funny?"

"You—white boy," one of the kids blurted, pointing directly at me.

They all burst into uncontrollable laughter. I walked away hurt and confused.

I didn't understand why they were calling me a white boy when I clearly was black.

I started asking around and finally learned they were calling me a white boy because I used correct English and grammar instead of slang.

Their mockery made me deeply insecure, and I started to believe something was wrong with me.

I started to hate the way I talked, looked and laughed. My insecurity and self-hatred intensified when the kids in my school started judging the looks of the opposite sex. Every couple of weeks the boys would write down a grade for how attractive they thought the girls were, and the girls would do the same for the boys. If they thought you were attractive, you would get an A. If they thought you weren't attractive, you would get a D. One day as I was walking down our school's hallway, I found a paper with the guys' grades on it and saw a D next to my name from almost every black girl in my grade.

I didn't understand why my appearance grades were so low. I thought I looked nice enough to at least get some B's. But then I found out the girls thought my clothes were sloppy and out of style. They didn't like that I "talked white," and they saw me as too dark-skinned. According to them, I was overall lame and boring.

Hearing those opinions made me go from hating my personality to hating my image. They were right. I did dress sloppy. All of my clothes were two sizes too big because I was tall and consistently outgrew my clothes every year. Because my mom couldn't afford to keep buying me new clothes, she bought them two sizes too big so I could keep them for awhile.

I was one of the darkest-skinned people in my grade. Every time the lights went out at school the somebody would shout, "Hey, where'd Darryll go?" Then everyone would burst out laughing.

Also, I was kind of lame and boring by their standards. They partied. I studied. They skipped class. I had perfect attendance. They hung out in the hallways and clowned. I volunteered for the school credit union. When they joked, everyone laughed. When I joked, no one got it.

I didn't understand why I wasn't funny. I couldn't help that I couldn't afford stylish clothes, and even if I could, I had no sense of fashion.

My white friends never had a problem with me, though, except when it came time to visit my house in the 'hood. No one would do that. Their homes were so much better. They had guest bedrooms, fancy dining rooms, comfortable living rooms with sectional couches, new carpet, central AC, hardwood floors and safe neighborhoods.

I had nails coming up through my dusty hardwood floors, no carpet, no dining room, no living room, no couch, an old-fashioned floor cyclone fan for AC and a trap (drug) house across the street.

I was good enough to hang around as long as I went to them. I didn't have a problem with that at first. I knew their houses were better options. I preferred them, in fact. But things changed in the seventh grade when my cousin Chas moved in with me after his mom was shot and murdered in broad daylight.

Chas was the complete opposite of me.

He grew up in the projects, which were much more dangerous than my neighborhood. At that age, Chas was already skipping school, getting in fights, trying to have sex with girls and was exposed to or involved with plenty of drug and other illegal activities.

Chas was well-respected by the black community. He was charismatic, funny and fashionable, even though he was poor. Chas received a majority of A's and B's on the appearance report cards.

Chas had a completely different group of friends.

My friends were all white, except the other black kid who I had known since the third grade. My friends attended school regularly, earned good grades, ate family dinners and, at worst, got drunk at their parents' house under their supervision. Yes, that's bad behavior, but it's nothing compared to what Chas' friends were involved in.

Chas' friends got in fights all the time, carried weapons, smoked and sold weed, and some were already dropping out of school.

Chas' friends came by our house all the time. They stayed the night. Played video games. Rapped with us. They made fun of me for talking white and thought I was lame and "bummy." The only reason they hung out with me was because I was Chas' cousin. I was happy to be included, though.

Part of me liked being around my white friends, who liked me for me. The other part of me loved being around Chas' friends because they came to my neighborhood and my house.

I reached the point of having to choose between my friends—white or black.

The racial tension and differences were too vast to be friends with both groups. I got tired of telling my white friends that I couldn't go to their party because my black friends were having one. I got sick of feeling conflicted about which table I joined in the lunchroom.

Because I was black, I chose the black friends.

At that point, I started to pretend like I never knew my white friends. I deleted their numbers. I walked past them in the hallways like I'd never met them. I withdrew from my accelerated classes to get away from them. Even worse, I started changing everything about myself to gain the approval of the black community.

I took fashion tips from Chas. I started skipping school, smoking and selling weed, only dating black girls and fighting. I was nearly expelled from school and started talking slang instead of using proper grammar. I even changed how I laughed.

My efforts worked. The black community started respecting me. They invited me to exclusive parties, and I even got a GPA boost on the appearance reports from the girls. Instead of D's, I started getting B's and C's, and yes, even one A.

Yet, the more I fit in with the black community, the more I lost sight of my true self.

I knew my behavior was a pretend show my friends believed was real. I was pretending to be like them, even though deep down inside, I wasn't like them. In fact, I didn't even really like them.

I knew that if I were truly myself, they wouldn't like me either.

Yet, as time went on, I realized there were some things about "black life" that did feel true to who I was and what I liked: the food, the movies, the jokes and more. I was conflicted. I didn't know who I was anymore. I wanted people to like me for me—not because I acted like them. I wanted them to invite me to parties because they wanted me there—not because I talked, dressed and behaved like them.

Enter the world of sports. And the granting of my wish.

Toward the end of eighth grade, I started excelling at sports. I had always been decent, mainly because I was tall. But by the time my growth slowed in eighth grade, my coordination started to catch up with my height.

I started playing travel basketball and spent more time training with my father, who had been a star Division I athlete and was on track to play professionally were it not for a career-ending knee injury. Sound familiar? Like father, like son, I guess.

Once I got to high school and started dominating in track and field, basketball and football, media wrote about me, and people—black, white, young and old—began talking to me all the time about my games and sports life.

I no longer felt I had to choose between black friends and white friends. Sports was something everyone could relate to. I could tell my lame jokes and still get invited to the black parties ... because I was a star athlete. I could talk white or talk black, smoke weed or drink alcohol, play beer pong or shoot craps and not get made fun of ... because I was a star athlete. Sports became the reason I was respected, accepted and loved. Not only did sports bring me friendship, but I also fell in love with the disciplined schedule, the intense physical and mental demands and, of course, the attention.

The newspaper articles, the fans cheering "MVP" when I shot free throws, the girls (who now gave me A's) wanting to date me, and all of the people who wanted my autograph was exhilarating. I was accepted for the first time since third grade, and I never wanted it to end. All I wanted was more. More fame. More fans. More money. More girls. More friends. More power. More esteem. More accolades. More praise. More attention. More applause. More everything.

Sports was my vehicle to all of this. That's why I signed with Central Michigan University to play football and basketball. I wanted to make history as one of the first to play not just professional basketball and football, but to DOMINATE both sports. I wanted to set records that would never be broken.

A lot of people my age said they wanted to "be like Mike," (Michael Jordan). I wanted to be better than Mike. I wanted people to hear the name Darryll or Stints, as they would call me, and say, "He's the greatest athlete of all time."

My dream of dominating both sports professionally was shattered when my football coaches realized they could use me my freshman year and weren't going to redshirt me. The coaches decided it was best for me not to play basketball so I wouldn't get hurt for football. The CMU head basketball coach and I fussed and complained, but we couldn't do much because the football program was paying my scholarship.

I was crushed because basketball was my first love. But I found peace from the dozens of coaches and mentors who told me it was much more likely that I would dominate in football rather than basketball based on my height.

So, I set my mind to becoming the greatest football player ever. That was the end goal. My first step was to break all of Dan Bazuin's defensive records at CMU. This was an easy short-term goal in my mind because I watched Bazuin play, and I knew I was more athletic and much faster than he was. The strength and knowledge of the game were all I needed to shatter his records.

My plan suffered a rude awakening when I ruptured a disc in my back while squatting improperly during a workout in the winter of my freshman year. The injury eventually required emergency surgery to save my left leg from becoming paralyzed due to a prolonged pinched nerve. My coaches, trainers and teammates were astonished. The athletic department agreed to honor all four years of my scholarship. Everyone told me to have the surgery and be grateful that I could focus on my education and career beyond sports without the strenuous demands that came from playing football.

The problem was that being an athlete wasn't just something I did—it had become who I was. It wasn't just my dream—it had become my identity. It was the thing that gave me popularity and acceptance. It was why people knew me. It was how I was supposed to make a name for myself in the world. It had become the foundation of all of my relationships. It couldn't be over. Not so soon. Not without me becoming the best player of all time. Not before breaking Bazuin's records. Without sports, who was I? I had no desire to do anything else. I thought being done with sports meant being done with life. And, I couldn't be done with life. Not yet.

So, I decided to defy the odds. Instead of accepting that my back injury would be the end of my athletic career, I decided to make a comeback. I had the surgery and put myself through intense physical discipline to get into top physical shape.

I didn't obey the post-surgery, six-month rest requirement and started immediately rehabilitating and training the day after my surgery. I ignored my body's pain signals by taking extra painkillers. I found a way to deceive the healthcare system and medical professionals so I could get illegal doses of epidural shots and more subscriptions for opioids and access to medical marijuana. Since neither the football program nor my personal health insurance would cover the cost of my medical expenses and medical frauds, I started selling drugs (mostly weed and Adderall) throughout Michigan to cover my healthcare expenses. Through self-will, illegal procedures, painkillers and a lot of lies to my athletic trainers, coaches and doctors, I earned a starting position as defensive end within six months of my surgery.

I competed for two years while hiding my pain and continuing my drug abuse/addiction. Toward the end of my junior season, the coaches started to catch on to me because I was losing my ability to stand up straight, and I kept having frequent nosebleeds. I told them the nosebleeds were caused by my allergies. In reality, too many opioids were thinning my blood to the point that every time I made contact on the field, my nose would bleed. I hid the nose bleeds by using nose plugs, but it was becoming impossible to hide the physical effects of the pain. Not only was I bent over, but I also was limping because of the tension between my lower back and hamstrings. I would often avoid any head-on collision on the field, which if you understand football, you know that's a huge no-no.

Our athletic trainers and coaches agreed they needed to kick me off the team. They wanted to protect me from further injury, even though they were not liable for them due to my signed liability waiver.

I remember when they told me the news. "Stinson," the head athletic trainer said despondently after pulling me aside and barely making eye contact. "We appreciate everything you have done for this team, but we can't watch you do this to yourself anymore, Darryll. We know something is wrong, and we need to let you go." Hearing those words felt so unreal.

He continued.

"We know you love the team and have put your body on the ..."

I stormed out.

I couldn't hear them tell me it was over. They hadn't believed I could come back to play again in the first place. Who were they to tell me I couldn't find a way to overcome my physical limitations?

"I'll prove them wrong again!" I thought.

Yet deep down, I knew they were right this time. I had tried just about everything I could to keep my career alive. Surgery, acupuncture, nerve killings, epidural shots, chiropractic care, physical therapy, traction, yoga, back braces, custom soles, prayer, anti-inflammatory medicine, muscle relaxers and close to a hundred other treatment options.

None of it worked. I had to face the reality that my athletic career was finished. I didn't know who I was outside of sports. I had spent my entire life since the third grade being someone I wasn't. I had allowed other people and my athletic ability to define who I was. At this point in my life, I didn't know which laugh was authentically mine, what music I really liked, or how I preferred to talk. But the one thing I was sure of was that I loved playing sports.

I wasn't good at anything else. I didn't like anything else. I didn't want anything else. I wanted to play sports because it was my life.

I had experienced the loneliness, depression and pointlessness of life during my short time of not playing sports while I was rehabbing after my back surgery. I overcame those struggles because the hope of playing again motivated me. This time I would have to face those emotions without the hope and motivation of being able to play again.

I had no desire to live. There was just no point. Yes, I had family. A very caring and supportive family.

But they didn't really know me. I didn't even know me. And the depression I was facing was so dark and heavy I didn't care what they would think if I killed myself.

I had a girlfriend whom I had been dating for four and a half years who consoled me, initially. The hope of marrying her was the only reason I didn't harm myself in the beginning of my battle with depression. However, once I wasn't headed to the NFL anymore, she left me and got engaged to another man.

Her leaving further proved my belief that without sports, I wasn't any good to anybody. In her defense, I don't blame her for leaving because our relationship had been so unhealthy, including my cheating over the years. I know now she made the right choice. But in the moment, it was devastating.

She was the only one I would ever open up to about my suicidal thoughts. I was too embarrassed to share with anyone else. I would throw hints at my mom and my pastor, but not enough for them to know I was serious.

I didn't want to talk to anyone. I just wanted to disappear.

I started making attempts to end my life. One day, I swallowed an entire bottle of Vicodin in hopes that I would never wake up. When overdosing on pain pills didn't work, I mixed them with alcohol. When that didn't work, I tried living recklessly. Multiples times, I drank nearly a fifth of alcohol, smoked multiple blunts and swallowed a variety of pills before I got in my car to drive. My goal was that I would be so high and intoxicated that I would get in a tragic life-ending accident.

I wanted so badly for somebody to just take my life for me. I wanted a semi to lose control and kill me dead in the street. I wanted someone from my drug transactions to get greedy, rob and shoot me to death. I didn't have the "courage" to shoot or hang myself. I didn't have the "guts" to jump in front of a truck or out of a building.

So, I tried starving myself. I went from 275 pounds to 219 pounds in four weeks from barely eating. But even that wasn't enough to end it all.

I decided to do something I knew I couldn't survive. I planned to steer my car into oncoming traffic the next time I got in my vehicle. I took as many drugs as I could while sitting inside my car in a vacant parking lot. I wrote my suicide letter, started crying as I finished what would be my last blunt.

I turned my phone on silent and started speeding 75 mph down a 35-mph road headed toward the highway and ultimately oncoming traffic. I share the rest of this story in the chapter "What Really Happened?" You can find out the rest of the details there.

This attempted suicide is what landed me in the psychiatric unit at Henry Ford Hospital. And it was all because my athletic career had come to an end.

That's how it happened.

That's how I went from living the "good life" to wanting to end my life.

I must take a moment to say if you think your life is meaningless just because your athletic career is finished, you're wrong. There's life after sports. There's very real hope. There's more to you than how high you can jump, how fast you can run or how well you can perform. The fact that you're reading this means there's breath in your lungs. And as long as you're still breathing, there's still a purpose for you.

I want to clarify that when I mentioned earlier that I did not have the courage to shoot myself or the guts to jump out of a building, I was speaking from the frame of mind that I had in that moment, not how I perceive that situation now.

Taking your life is not courageous. Staying alive when everything in you wants to quit is.

I'll also say that clinical depression is real. I was diagnosed with it. I've been prescribed antidepressants and psychiatric care. Don't feel bad or ashamed if you need medicine to deal with your depression, anxiety or other mental illnesses. I'd rather you get help than suffer in silence. Further, there is no shame in seeing a counselor or psychiatrist. I still do. Some athletes struggle to communicate their emotions. We typically bottle up our emotional life or use sports as the outlet of our pain. We may be successful at hiding the pain, but just because we hide it doesn't mean it's not there.

It's OK not to be OK. Please talk to someone about it. Write a note or send a text if you struggle to verbalize your feelings. But please don't isolate yourself and keep your emotions to yourself because you think you're being tough. Even if you think what you're going through is small and not that big of a deal—TALK about it. Depression grows in silence and multiplies in isolation.

One of the quickest ways to get rid of the darkness of depression is to break the silence and turn on the light.

I apologize if these comments come off harsh or insensitive. That is not the heart with which I write them. I want to offer hope and practical tips when dealing with depression before moving forward with our life-after-sports strategies.

I'm sharing words of hope and insight that I wish I would have heard while facing the monster of depression. Depression affects millions of people across the world, and I will not allow it to have its way with you or anyone else who reads this book.

Depression from the end of my athletic career almost cost me my life, my purpose, my wife, my children and my future.

Fortunately, I had a life-changing experience in that psychiatric unit that gave me hope that my life had purpose. You can read the chapter "What Really Happened?" to get the full story.

The next three to five years after being released from Henry Ford were challenging. I knew I had a reason to live because of what happened there, but I couldn't quite figure out what that reason was. Additionally, I still missed being an athlete and was sick of people telling me to find something I was passionate about when I wasn't passionate about anything other than sports!

Eventually, I came to an amazing place. I finally found fulfillment in who I was without having the title of athlete. Truth be told, I became more excited about my future than I was about my former sports career. I could watch sports and not feel the need to talk about my athletic accolades. I was motivated to work out by something other than winning a game. It took time, but it became an awesome reality.

I've been able now to reflect on my journey and the milestones that helped me clarify my identity, discover my purpose, live fulfilled and reach the top of my industry. I've narrowed my transition process to five steps or phases, which I call The Athlete Transition Roadmap, a proven framework to help you discover new purpose and create a future you'll love more than your past.

In this book, you'll read what took me five years to learn.

My hope is that this book will shorten the gap for you. Time is precious, and there's not just life after sports, there's purpose after sports.

It doesn't matter if you're a current or former athlete, military veteran or retired corporate executive. Whether you know what you want to do with the rest of your life, have no clue about what's next, or already are building your new life, this book can help you move toward greater impact and fulfillment.

Roadmap: How do you learn to accept you're no longer an elite athlete?

Despite the condition of my back, I wanted nothing more than to be a professional athlete. After my life-changing encounter in the psychiatric unit, I knew my life had a purpose beyond sports. Yet the further away I got from that enlightening experience, the more my love and desire to play sports began to dominate my thoughts. These thoughts inspired me to want to try to compete at the highest level again. I started doing rehab exercises and working out. I was determined to get into top physical shape, show up at the next NFL Pro Day at my university and shock everyone with my exemplary performance. I imagined the looks on my coaches' faces when they saw me walk into the indoor football stadium to start stretching. I could feel the handshakes and chest bumps from teammates who were excited to see me on the field again. I felt myself running the fastest 40, the fastest 4-cone drill and jumping the highest vertical for my position group and even some of the skill positions. I pictured myself being interviewed by ESPN as they highlighted my comeback story. I envisioned myself on the Dallas Cowboys football field, looking into the empty stands after signing my NFL contract, and feeling such a deep heart-warming sense of accomplishment. It was all so real in my mind that you couldn't tell me my life story wasn't meant to be written this way.

Yet, the harder I worked out, the more my back ached. Many times, I would work out hard for two or three days and then have to wait another week to work out so my back could recover.

One night, after feeling one of my many overwhelming inspirations to train, I jumped the football stadium fence at CMU to work out on the field beneath the stadium lights. I started practicing on the defensive line dummies to see what it felt like to push some weight around. I felt amazing, like my old pre-back surgery self for a moment until I twisted the wrong way, had an intense back spasm that sent sharp pains down my legs causing me to instantly fall to the ground. I lay there with my hands beneath my back, gazing into the sky wondering what else I could do to make a comeback. I was convinced that there had to be a medical treatment, an exercise, a surgery I hadn't tried.

Then came another one of my bright ideas. I'll just play basketball! It always had been my first love anyway. This was perfect because basketball would be less demanding on my back than football. I wouldn't have to push around 300-pound linemen or collide with anyone running at full speed. And, I wouldn't have to worry nearly as much about concussions that could lead to paralysis from my spinal condition. So, I rolled over, clenched my abs tightly and got up from the ground. It took a week of rehabbing and icing my back every 20 minutes to be painless enough to work out again. But as soon as I felt 50 percent, I hit the basketball court early in the morning to get after it.

The first practice felt great. My ball handling skills were a little rusty, but my shot was still on point, and my hops were off the charts. All my football leg workouts were clearly paying off. I was jumping higher than I ever had before, and I felt amazing doing trick dunks. I left the court that day with great hope and anticipation that everything I went through was for me to return to my first love of basketball again.

I remember thinking, "This is it. This is what I was supposed to be doing all along anyways!" I began rehearsing my comeback success story. I could hear people comparing me to Jordan and how he got cut from his high school team yet ended up being the greatest basketball player of all time. I saw myself in the NBA, stealing the ball from (the late) Kobe Bryant and scoring 30 points on Lebron James. I couldn't wait to continue training.

I set my alarm for 5 a.m. and went to bed with that giddy butterflies in your stomach feeling kids have on Christmas Eve.

My alarm went off around 5 a.m. I was so excited to get up and get after it. I tried to jump out of bed, but ... wait... somehow... I couldn't move. It felt like my back was strapped to the mattress. When I tried to roll over, I felt extreme sharp pains shoot up both sides of my spine.

I placed my hand on my back and could feel the swelling, no doubt caused by all the jumping and dunks I had done the day before.

Completely frustrated and holding back tears of anger, I cried out to God and begged Him to heal my back. I vowed that I would never do anything bad again. I promised I would give a ton of money to the poor if He would just take away my pain. I tried deal after deal to bargain with God. But nothing happened. No miraculous healing. No relief of pain. No decreased swelling. Just a nagging, constant reminder that no matter how badly I wanted to play, my career was finished. Having already gone through drug addiction and depression to continue playing football my sophomore and junior year, I knew continuing to pursue a career in sports despite my back injury wasn't a wise option. There was no way I was going through that again.

I knew I had to learn to accept that my career was finished. I just didn't know how.

All athletes face this reality at some point, no matter how talented they are. At some point, every one of us will have to hang up the cleats, set down the gloves and throw away the running shoes. Forced or by choice, the end of our athletic career is inevitable and unavoidable.

That means that we have to learn to accept it—in our minds and in our hearts—so we can move forward in our lives. There's a big difference between athletes who've accepted that their career is done in their minds and those who've accepted it in their hearts. I know a lot of athletes who mentally accepted the end of their career. They found jobs and started families, but their hearts still desire to be athletes. To them, there's nothing more fulfilling than being a star athlete. Which means they exist day-to-day, viewing their current life as second best.

They might even have highly successful careers. Yet, if they had the chance to play sports again, they would in a heartbeat. These are the former athletes who compete obsessively in everyday life. They can't stand to lose, not even to their kids or their spouse. And they talk about their athletic careers endlessly.

Some of them train and train and train like they're going to make a comeback, while everyone watching their social media posts knows they need to give it up and move forward with their lives.

Some get depressed, like I did, and turn to drugs, pornography, cutting, or some other destructive habit. Some won't even entertain a conversation about it because the loss of status, attention and the mojo they had as athletes hurts too much.

Hard stop. Think about this. Can you ever have a fully satisfied life if you would trade your present for your past? That's like a husband in his second marriage saying, "Hey, baby. I love you and am happy, but if my ex-wife ever wants to get back together, I'd leave you in a heartbeat."

Chances are that marriage would not last long. It would be uncomfortable and lackluster at best.

I don't want you to live that way. I want you to be fulfilled, loving your life just as much or more than when you were an athlete. I want you to be just as energized, fired up, driven and happy as when you were competing at a high level.

The only way for you to do that is to allow yourself to feel and process the full weight and spectrum of your emotions associated with the end of your athletic career.

You might have to cry multiple times, pray or seek counseling, but do whatever it takes to come to that place of acceptance. Accepting that your career is finished does not mean you can't talk at times about your memories, the plays you made, or how you miss the game. **Acceptance, when it's complete, means you no longer have an overwhelming desire to become or continue to be an athlete.**

This was very difficult for me. People admire athletes even if they don't know them. Successful athletes often have a massive social media following. One of my former teammates went from 1,000 social media followers to more than 1 million within a week of becoming a professional athlete. I wanted that influence and craved that adoration.

And then there are the financial perks. Pro athletes can make substantial salaries and have the potential for additional income through endorsements, commercials, apparel and more. I wanted that income. I wanted those endorsements. Having lived my entire life without enough money personally or in my family to do what we wanted, how we wanted, when we wanted, a sports career was my answer to financial success.

Plus, I loved the game. I loved outperforming my opponent. I loved the idea of getting paid to work out and master the game. I got butterflies in my stomach knowing that as a professional athlete, I would not have to sit behind a desk all day, check email and go to boring meetings where nobody gets anything done. I wanted to get paid to listen to music while working out, play games, sign autographs, travel and film commercials. Oh yeah, and since I love connecting with people, I was ecstatic about opportunities to meet people and other superstars from across the world. I'm embarrassed to admit this, but at that time, I dreamed of being able to choose any woman I wanted to be my spouse. I had a mental list of actresses and models whom I'd pursue once I won the NFL defensive rookie of the year award.

My adoration of the career of a professional athlete made this acceptance phase extremely challenging for me. Simply put, nothing else measured up to the perks of being a pro athlete. I knew I could be successful in other careers, but I just didn't want to.

Even though I was experiencing success in my current job, I was not satisfied. I would come home from work and try to drink or smoke my sorrow away. I would watch old films of my playing sports and dream about becoming a professional athlete. I would cry in my counseling sessions.

Compounding it all was that I couldn't even enjoy casual sports. Basketball, football, bowling, soccer and boxing all required the use of my broken lower back. I could barely play billiards without ibuprofen.

A few times I considered again taking my life, but because of what happened at the psychiatric unit in Detroit, I knew deep inside that I was alive for a purpose, and it wasn't sports. I knew there had to be a way for me to get rid of this tormenting desire to be an athlete. I knew I couldn't be happy climbing the corporate ladder when I would give my soul in a second to play sports again. There had to be something I could do to have a change of heart.

There was.

Acceptance begins when idolizing ends

To idolize something means to worship it as a god. I discovered that at some point along my journey, I shifted from wanting to become a professional athlete to idolizing the profession. That's an important concept. As a kid, I just wanted to play the game. It was less about money and status. However, my ego grew in proportion to media attention, fans chanting my name, special attention from coaches, teachers and business owners, and people who knew who I was even though I had no clue who they were. It all got to my head. It made me feel special. It made me feel better than other people. It made me feel like... well... a god.

I can't tell you exactly when it happened. But one day, I had an epiphany that if I felt loved, validated and respected because of sports, my desires were all jacked up. I realized something was wrong if I felt like a nobody just because I had a career change. I realized sports had become who I was versus what I did, and I could see that losing sports had somehow equated to losing myself. That was a pivotal moment in my journey. I realized that I needed to make a conscious decision to separate my identity from my career. I had to separate external success from internal satisfaction.

As I was making the subconscious decision to stop idolizing sports, hope began to rise within me. I knew the less I saw sports as a god that held my future and my happiness, the easier it would be to move on toward personal fulfillment.

If this is where you are, I want to encourage you by telling you that sports are not your everything. They're awesome. They're amazing. They're wonderful. Play as hard as you can for as long as you can to become the best that you can. But don't allow sports to become your identity. Don't you dare think that because sports are not in your life anymore, you can't be loved and respected. Because as you'll learn throughout this book, you are more than an athlete. You are more than how high you can jump or how fast you can run. You are more than a soccer player, more than an MVP, more than a hall of famer.

You are somebody, whether you have a title or not. You are the character that you display. You are the values that you hold dear. So, take sports off the throne of your heart. Sports are a game, or for some a career, but they are not a god worth idolizing.

Embrace gratitude

Viewing sports as a career and not as a god helped me to move closer to truly accepting the end of my athletic career. It made it easier for me to cope with the depression that came from not being able to compete. Yet, part of me remained mad, frustrated and angry. I became furious as I mentally rehearsed all the tackles I missed and games I lost. I wanted so badly to go back and change all of my mistakes. But I couldn't. And not being able to gnawed at me. I had a poor attitude about life, until one day I heard a public speaker say, "Your gratitude determines your attitude, and your attitude determines your altitude."

Uh-oh. That statement made me realize just how ungrateful I truly was. Many times, all I thought about were the mistakes I made, the poor decisions coaches made, how the NCAA didn't really care about the players, and how the administrators were all money-hungry jerks who only liked me for my athletic ability and not for me as a person. I wasn't just ungrateful, I was bitter. And I was challenged to find things to be grateful for, even in the worst situations.

I started thinking about my life, my relationships, my opportunities and my surroundings and chose to focus on the beauty of life instead of the blemishes.

Here are some areas where I started to practice gratitude.

1. **My life**. People die every day. I started appreciating that I wasn't one of them, especially knowing former teammates who lost their lives due to the pressures that come with athletic transition.

2. **My health.** Despite my back injury, and whatever damage came from my drug addiction, I was in good health. I could see, walk and talk. That's a privilege not everyone has. I wondered what someone in a wheelchair would think if they heard me complaining about my sports injury. I realized my health was still a blessing, even if it didn't come with the perk of being a physical phenomenon.

3. **My friends and family**. I once heard a true story of a guy who was so lonely, he bought a dog and named him "Friend." I know students who have taken their lives thinking no one wanted to be their friend. I felt lonely many times after my sports career ended and complained that no one understood me. But

there's a big difference between feeling lonely and being alone. I realized the only reason I felt alone was that I wasn't talking to people around me. I was isolating myself and feeling like no one cared. It was a lie. People did care. I had plenty of friends and family. Even if you have just one friend or family member to talk to, you're doing better than some. It's a reason to be thankful.

4. **My athletic experiences.** It was a huge boost to my mental health when I started to be grateful for what I experienced as an athlete rather than regretful for what I didn't get to do. I became grateful that sports allowed me to travel across America, fly on a private jet, play on national television with or against some of the top athletes in the world, meet people I never would have met otherwise, and earn a college degree nearly debt-free. That's a lot to be thankful for!

5. **My current life situation.** One of my favorite sayings now is, "Be careful when you complain because someone in the world is praying to be you." It reminds me that no matter how bad my current circumstances are, there are people who would swap places with me in a heartbeat.

Practicing gratitude helped me to fight depression and move to a healthier place of acceptance.

Yet (you know what's coming, don't you?) every so often I'd have these nagging thoughts that would argue back while I was trying to be grateful. Thoughts such as, "So, you played with some of the best athletes in the world. You aren't one of them!" or, "Stop pretending you don't miss sports when you're not making anywhere near as much as you could have been."

Negative thoughts like these warred against my gratitude constantly. Thankfully, my eyes were opened when I had an opportunity to work with Central Michigan University's athletic communications department as an unpaid assistant. My responsibilities were to interview coaches for pre- and post-game quotes, transport stat sheets from the press box to the field and call the play-by-play for ESPN's internal communication team. These duties helped me see a bigger and more beautiful scene taking place around the athletes. I never noticed what was happening around me when I was an athlete; I had tunnel vision. All I thought about was playing well and winning games. I may have waved at the fans and my family, but I was so focused on the game that I missed the energy that surrounded me.

In the communications role, I saw friends and disconnected families come together to watch a game. I saw people from different ethnicities come together to cheer on the team. I saw a community come to life because its home team was winning.

I had never appreciated any of that until this point. Before, all I had focused on was myself. But when I gained this new perspective, it gave me more to be grateful for and led me to a profound revelation: My entire athletic career had been focused on my status when it should have been focused on my impact. The impact I could make was far more important than my status because focusing on impact benefits more people than just myself. No one but me benefited from my status, but there were unlimited opportunities for those who could benefit from my service.

Here's how that was important to living my best life after sports. Had I been focused on impact, the transition out of sports would have been much easier because my opportunity for impact would be alive and well. Would I have less money? Probably. Fewer followers? More than likely. Less impact? Not at all. I could still have impact! Focusing on impact instead of status helped me release the part of me that still wanted to be an athlete for success and fame. It helped me loosen the grip on my desire to play sports because now I could appreciate the people, places and things around me and begin to see opportunities to impact others.

Accept accomplishments and let go of past potential

One factor that made adjusting to life after athletics so hard was that I never reached my athletic peak or prime. As I mentioned in the introduction chapter, "What Happened," I endured back surgery at the end of my true freshman year of college.

One day as I was squatting heavy weight, I ruptured a disc in my back. I went the entire summer without seeing a specialist because I was athletic enough to still lead sprints and play well, even though I had serious back issues. Toward the end of that summer, I started to notice something was seriously wrong. My left leg was throbbing, and it looked a lot skinnier than my right leg. I would wake up in the middle of the night in excruciating pain. This went on for a few weeks and progressed to the point where I had to take Vicodin and prop my leg at a 90-degree angle at night against my windowpane just to get some decent sleep. Within a week, I noticed further, rapid deterioration of muscles in my left leg.

Finally, I went to a back specialist and was shocked at the news he shared after reviewing my X-rays and MRI. He told me I had severe degenerative disc disease, multiple bulging discs and a badly pinched nerve that was causing the muscle deterioration. He was concerned that if I didn't have surgery soon, my left leg would end up paralyzed. Although he was booked for the next six months, the doctor really cared about his patients and offered to come in on his day off to perform my surgery. His name was Dr. Gerald Schell, from Saginaw, Michigan. And, yes, that is a shameless plug.

The surgery was pretty simple. He would cut me open, shave off the part of my disc that was pinching my nerve, move the disc a little and sew me back up. Dr. Schell couldn't promise I would play again, but he did say it was possible. That's all I needed to hear!

My coaches and athletic trainers saw my situation differently. They suggested I focus on my education and leave sports alone. I would never forget the words of our head athletic trainer, Phillip J. Adler, who said, "Darryll. It's not about whether you can come back and play. It's about whether you should come back and play. You want to be able to hold your daughter one day—don't you?" (The irony is I have three daughters now. Maybe Phillip was a prophet of some sort. Lol.)

What's more, one of my teammates had the same surgery a year earlier. He worked hard to get back on the field but was only making his back worse. He had decided to focus on his education.

I was too committed to sports to do that. In fact, the more people told me the odds of someone playing in the NFL after back surgery, the more determined I became to defy the odds. Our athletic administrators promised to honor my four-year scholarship and allow me to be around the team whenever I wanted. Sounds like a good deal, right? I would receive a full-ride scholarship, could focus on my education and be around football whenever I wanted. I didn't have to wake up early for workouts, stay up late to watch film, or fight sleep during team meetings. And I still would get to attend the games, eat the meals and get championship rings. Sweet!

Not! I had been told all my life that I had the potential to become a great professional athlete. My freshman year, a coach who worked with NFL athletes told me it was not a matter of if I would play professionally, it was a matter of when. So, giving up was not an option. I was determined to be the best athlete of all time. I rejected the offer to focus on school and not play football. The coaches and trainers were shocked that I would put my body at such great risk. They knew the chances of me playing college football after a back surgery were slim to none. And they went from offering me a choice not to play to telling me they were not going to allow me to play. Despite the warnings, I persisted. I cried and begged and cried and begged until finally, the coaches and trainers agreed to let me try to get cleared to play again as long as I signed a liability waiver, which meant they would not be liable for any further injuries.

I signed the waiver. I had the surgery. Doctors told me to do nothing but take showers and lay down for two weeks. I made myself walk the day after my surgery. My insurance only covered six months of physical therapy and 20 chiropractic visits, which I used within two months, so I started paying for my rehabilitation out-of-pocket.

I used my leftover scholarship money, Pell grant money and money from family. That wasn't enough to cover chiropractic visits five times a week, acupuncture twice a month, physical therapy seven days a week and other expenses like gas, X-rays, food, vitamins, prescriptions, MRIs, custom shoe soles, back braces and additional rehabilitation equipment. So, in order to cover these expenses, I started selling drugs, primarily marijuana and Adderall across the state of Michigan. My life began to spiral out of control going from workouts, to drug transactions, to classes, to film sessions, to drug transactions to evening classes, to bed and repeat.

To make a long story short, I defied all the odds. I proved the coaches and trainers wrong. I did what few have ever done. I came back from surgery to not just play college football, but to earn a starting position within six months.

However, doing so came with a cost: My health. I was lying to doctors about my medical records so I could get more epidural shots. I would get a bloody nose almost every practice and game. I told my coaches, trainers and teammates it was bad allergies, dry weather or a rough play when in reality I was taking so many pain pills they were thinning my blood. I succeeded at lying because I was performing decently well and making some plays. I led all the conditioning for my position group. I was among the top of my team for bench, vertical jump, 20-yard cone drill, etc. I worked my way up to a 275-pound defensive end and clocked a hand-timed 4.5 40-yard dash during winter workouts.

Yet, my performance on the field was average at best. No matter how many pills I took or epidural shots I got, I still couldn't move like I needed to. My back ached in my defensive stance. I had sharp pains down my sides when I would change direction, which slowed me down. I couldn't extend my body fully, which made it easy for an offensive lineman to push me around. I couldn't reach top speed because of the tension between my lower back and my hamstrings. My legs were terribly weak and would tire easily. Don't get me wrong. I made some plays. There was a reason I was a starter. But my tackles were weak and sometimes embarrassing. I played safe, avoided piles as much as possible and stood straight up a lot during games to ease the pain in my lower back. I would often close my eyes to endure the pain of collision and sometimes missed easy tackles or sacks because of my eyes being closed.

Finally, in 2011, my medical shirt junior year, my coaches and trainers had enough. They knew something was wrong because I couldn't stand up straight. They terminated my liability waiver and told me I was welcome to still come around the team whenever I wanted. I was furious because I felt like they were taking my dream away from me. But, honestly, at that point, I was in so much pain, I didn't even fight them. I had tried my best and given the game everything I had. My heart. My mind. My blood. My sweat. My tears. And literally my life. Now I was done playing sports forever.

I share these details because I want you to know how badly I wanted to play sports. I want you to know how hard I worked to keep my athletic career going because if you can understand the depths of what I went through physically and mentally, then you can understand how heartbreaking and depressing it was that I never reached my full potential. The guy who had the body and potential of an NFL athlete never even made third team all-conference in the Mid-American Conference. The guy who was once a 275-pound defensive lineman couldn't throw his weight and strength around on the field.

Everything I could have been as an athlete, I never was. I was just the guy who could have, would have and should have been great. That's the hard truth. And that's what made this phase of acceptance so challenging. I knew, my teammates knew, that if I could have been healthy, I would have been a BADDD man. But I wasn't a bad man—I just had a bad back.

Letting go of your potential

I found myself trying to explain to everybody how good of an athlete I could have been. I would tell them about my best games and rare athleticism. I loved telling people the story about how I was fast enough to challenge Antonio Brown to a race and was competitive. The truth was that he blasted past me at the get off, but I gained ground when my long stride kicked in. Oh, and of course I would brag about the times I beat 2013 No. 1 NFL draft pick Eric Fisher in pass rush drills. I made sure everyone knew how good I could have been. It was pathetic. I would talk about how I was a "better" athlete than every professional athlete I played against—Eric Fisher, Frank Zombo, Draymond Green, Brandon Jennings and more. I told people who cared and those who didn't. I told athletes and non-athletes. I briefed people who asked about my sports career and people who didn't ask. Why? Because it helped me cope with the pain of it being over. Somehow telling other people about how I dunked on somebody who was in the pros or outperformed someone who was doing well in college made me feel as if I were still competing. I was subconsciously trying to trick myself into believing I had lived up to my potential.

Who's convincing whom?

That subconscious mind-game shifted when I started to hear my former teammates, competitors and fans affirm my potential. They began to tell me how good I was or could have been instead of me telling them. A former teammate would say something like, "Man, Stinson, I know it hurts to watch so and so play because you were better than them." One All-American college football player told me, "Man, you could have easily gone pro if you didn't get hurt." One of my distant friends who is a professional football player said, "You could have easily been playing pro, man." These words of affirmation were not coming from my mother, sisters or unathletic friends. These were credible athletes who were being serious—not polite, and they were saying exactly what I was trying to get other people to understand.

Then it hit me. It wasn't other people I was trying to convince—it was myself. I was trying to believe that I was a great athlete just because I had the potential to dominate in sports. But my potential was just that— potential—not achievements.

I had to accept that although I could have been a professional athlete, I was never going to be one. I had to accept that even though I beat Eric Fisher in some pass rush drills, he got drafted No. 1, and I watched him play from my couch at home. Yes, I put up solid points against Draymond Green during our preseason game in 2007, but he was playing pro basketball making millions, and I was struggling to pay the cable bill to watch him play.

It sounds harsh, but it was reality. In order to fully get rid of the desire to be a professional athlete, I had to force myself to be content with my accomplishments, let go of my potential and stop seeking affirmation. Every time I talked about my potential, I was talking about something I never reached, and that created regret. Regret was keeping me stuck in the past. On the contrary, when I talked about my accomplishments, it created satisfaction and excitement. That helped me heal and move forward. I learned to appreciate the plays I did make and let go of the plays I could have made. I learned to accept and be happy with my accomplishments and stop talking about the "should haves," "could haves" and "would haves."

Simple solutions are not always easy solutions

Letting go of my potential was a simple, but not easy, process. In fact, it was excruciatingly painful. I cried every time I thought about how I would never be able to play professionally. I had trouble sleeping because my mind would constantly brainstorm ideas of how I could find a way to continue my athletic career. I could not watch more than two minutes of a college or professional basketball or football game without getting nauseous, depressed or angry. I knew acceptance was the solution to moving forward with my life, but it was so challenging. I was frustrated because I felt that since I knew what I needed to do that acceptance should be easy. I really thought I would just spend five minutes meditating or just wake up one day and the nagging desire to be an athlete would be gone. That's when I learned that just because something is simple doesn't mean it will be easy.

I had to learn to control my tongue in order to stop talking about my athleticism so that I could come to a healthy place of acceptance. I started tracking how many times sports came up in conversation, and I made the decision not to talk about myself. I turned the process into a game and tried to have more wins than losses. If I had to compete, at least it was against myself and ultimately for myself. Even if someone asked me "Stints, didn't you play against so and so," I'd say something like, "Yeah, and it's awesome to see them playing pro now," instead of my usually bragging about me rant. The more I controlled my tongue and stopped myself from talking about my potential, the easier it was to come to a place of acceptance.

Accidental hater

Even though talking about how I was better than other athletes was only my way of coping with no longer being able to play sports, I realized I had unintentionally become a hater of other athletes.

Urban Dictionary defines a hater as "a person who simply cannot be happy for another person's success.[8] So rather than be happy, they make a point of exposing a flaw in that person."

Hater sounds like a harsh word. At first, I dismissed any evidence that I was becoming a hater. I wasn't jealous of former teammates and competitors for playing at a high level; I just wanted to be there with them! But as I began monitoring my words, I discovered that unintentionally I had become exactly that—a hater. And, I knew that hating on other athletes only delayed my own journey toward acceptance and freedom from pain. So, in response, I listed three symptoms of every hater to help me recognize when I was accidentally hating. My goal in sharing these is for you to be able to identify any of these symptoms in yourself, and if so, to find better ways to cope and not get stuck in your transition to acceptance process.

Three symptoms of a hater

Symptom 1: Haters always find a way to discredit another's accomplishments.

If Lebron James scores 50 points, haters will mention how he only scored that many points because of the poor skills of the guy guarding him.

If Alabama's college football team wins another national championship, haters will say it's because they manipulate the recruits to get the best players, or they pay the refs to cheat for them.

To the hater, Lebron's 50 points has nothing to do with his work ethic, knowledge of the game or dominance as an athlete. Alabama's championship has nothing to do with the excellence of the physical trainers, the coaching staff or the leaders on the team.

Why? Because haters always find a way to discredit someone's accomplishment.

As metal detectors are to metal, so haters are to flaws. Haters are experts at pointing out weaknesses instead of celebrating strengths.

Symptom 2: Haters are masters at making the conversation about them.

No matter where the conversation starts, haters make sure it ends on them.

A conversation could begin with people talking about how Jordan is better than LeBron, and somehow it transitions to talking about how many points the hater averaged his junior year in high school.

I remember watching the NFL combine with friends who were talking about a defensive lineman running a 4.7 40-yard dash. Somehow, we ended up talking about my 100-meter hurdle times from my senior year in high school. I have no clue how we got there. But haters always find a way to make the conversation about them.

Symptom 3: Haters love to gossip and talk bad about other people.

A.W. Momerie said it this way in 1888: "It is easier, no doubt, to talk about persons, because so many disagreeable remarks spontaneously occur to one. It is more difficult to talk about things and events, because this requires a certain amount of intelligence and reflection and information. If we are to talk of things, we must know something about them. And it is our duty to see that we do."[9]

Simply stated: "Great minds discuss ideas; average minds discuss events; small minds discuss people."— Henry Thomas Buckle.[10]

Haters gossip and talk bad about others because they fall into the trap of small-minded thinking. Bad-talking others makes them feel better about themselves. Every time I talked bad about a dumb play another athlete made, it made me feel superior because, in my mind, I would have made a better play.

Unfortunately, unlike sports commentators, I wasn't getting paid to talk about other athletes. Hating was just an overflow of what was going on in my heart. It was easier to gossip about other athletes than it was to accept my own reality.

I'm not saying that every time people talk about other athletes it's gossip. I still discuss coaching changes. I still watch "Sports Center" and debate about how Jordan was and always will be better than Lebron. However, this is not at all the same as talking about others to soothe your own ego. The difference is the intent of your heart.

Maybe you're reading this and noticing you've had a symptom or two of being a hater.

I know how you feel.

I'm painfully aware of these symptoms because I had all three!

Deep down, I was so angry at myself for getting injured that talking bad about people who were playing at the next level appeased me. The deception of hating, however, is that we feel better—but only in the short-term. In the long-term, hating magnifies our insecurities and creates a deeper hole on the inside.

The hater's cure

The quickest way to gain victory over being a hater is to stop hating and start celebrating. Instead of pointing out reasons why a person or a team didn't deserve to win, celebrate the reasons they did win. Instead of discrediting Lebron for scoring 50 points because of poor defense, let's celebrate the fact that he had a 50-point game.

Celebrating instead of hating accelerated my acceptance process. After years of talking about other players, I finally realized it wasn't helping me. It may have made me feel better in the moment, but soon after that I would spiral down a dark tunnel of depressive thoughts. This may sound cheesy, but the more I celebrated other's wins, the better I felt. I can't explain it thoroughly, but I can tell you it worked. The more I kept the focus off my athletic ability, the less I wanted to play sports. When I talked about how much better I was than certain athletes, I wanted to get out there and prove it. Not being able to do that made acceptance harder.

It's hard not to talk about how good you were, especially when people are praising athletes who are nowhere near as good as you were. But if you're going to fully get rid of that desire to play sports again, you've got to resist the urge to hate on other athletes.

No more athlete. No more attention.

Have you ever ignored your cell phone for a long time? You know that feeling you get when you finally check it and realize nobody texted, called or even emailed you? Doesn't that make you feel so unimportant? So unloved? Multiply that feeling by a hundred, and that's what I felt when I was no longer an athlete.

If you haven't played for awhile, you know what I mean. The more successful you are in the eyes of others, the more attention you get. I was used to the crowd cheering for me, fans asking for autographs, coaches checking on me, teammates hitting me up, reporters wanting to do interviews, community members giving me high-fives for a good game, scouts and agents reaching out and family members telling me how proud they were. Then my career ended, and so did all the attention.

No one asked if I had won my last game. There was no last game. No one celebrated my non-existent stats. Not a single person asked for my autograph. Hardly any of my coaches checked in on me. Fans cheered only for the new superstar of the team. Family members stopped reaching out because my sport was our only shared interest. I felt like I went from being "a some-body" to everybody to being "a nobody" to everyone. One moment I felt like a superstar. The next I felt like a ghost. I literally felt like I didn't exist.

I assumed that because people gave me less attention, they never truly cared about me in the first place. And, since they never really cared about me, then they wouldn't care if I was alive or dead. I wouldn't be missed, and I would no longer be in pain.

Let me pause here and say that if you feel that way, get help now. Call the suicide prevention hotline. Call a former teammate, coach or teacher. Text a family member. Give people a chance to love you. And don't dismiss their love because you think they're just being polite. Somebody cares about you. I do. I might not know you, but I care about you. Because I was you. I know what it's like to feel that death will erase the pain of life. I know what it feels like to be so angry at people who were fake toward you that you want to kill yourself to get back at them. I know what it's like to have a billion thoughts running through your mind, including, "I bet if I died, people would care then." I'm no stranger to depression. I know that darkness too well.

As a person who was fortunate enough to survive a suicidal state of mind, trust me when I say your life is worth living. You might not believe it, but please borrow my belief. Sometimes you have to borrow somebody else's belief in you for awhile until you start believing in yourself. I believe in you. Your life is worth living. The pain you're feeling now, although deep, is temporary. It will pass with time and with help. Reach out to somebody.

If you've already tried talking to someone, and it didn't help, I've been there, too. I tried talking to family members, teammates, my girlfriend and pastor, and many times it seemed like they just made it worse. Sometimes, I got even more angry because I opened myself up, and people couldn't understand my pain. Some people even made me feel bad ... for feeling bad. If you're there, you've got to keep trying. Suicidal thoughts intensify in silence; they get stronger in isolation. The more you keep to yourself, the harder it will get. You've got to continue sharing your mental challenges with others so they can fight with you. Reach out to my team if you don't feel like anyone else will understand. We're here to help. You're not alone. You will get through this season and live to experience the greatness that's inside you!

Here's a life-after-sports power principle: Never interpret a lack of attention from others to mean that you lack worth. You're valuable whether people ask for your autograph or not. You're cherished whether you have fans or not. Your worth is not connected to your popularity, and it's not contingent, determined or dependent on what other people think about you. You are valuable because you're gifted. You're precious because you're unique. Even if you're a twin, there will never be anyone just like you. People don't have to like you, respect you or notice you for you to feel valuable and know that your life matters. People can hate on you; but that doesn't change your value. A $20 bill is worth $20 no matter what it's been through. It's the same for you. You might have made some mistakes. You might have been talked about. People who used to care about you when you played sports may not care about you now; but that doesn't change your value.

One discovery that helped me cope with the attention drop after my sports career ended was evaluating people who used to love me and brainstorming reasons why they no longer were interested in me. I landed on a process I call Fan Forgiveness.

I realized there were four types of fans.

- **The bandwagoners:** These were people who only liked me, talked to me, followed me and coached me because I was good at sports. After my career ended, they found a different player to support. They weren't friends to begin with, so there was no reason for me to get depressed because of their disloyalty.
- **The businesspersons:** These are the coaches, agents, media, administrators, bosses, etc. whose interest in me was business only. They saw me as a business investment instead of a human being. To them, there wasn't much difference between me and a capital stock. I realize that once you reach a certain talent level, sports become a business. There's no value in holding grudges and becoming bitter. I had to learn to stop taking their exit from my life so personal. Business is business. As a businessman myself, I could understand why

they wouldn't pour time or money into someone who couldn't produce a return on their investment. I'm not saying I agree with their beliefs, but relating to them was the best way to release the bitterness from my heart and help me move forward on my journey to acceptance.

- **The admirers:** These are family members, friends and teachers who just didn't know what to talk to me about beyond sports. Seriously, someone once asked me how football was going five years after my career ended. Even when I explained that I was done playing and had moved into a new career, they continued asking me questions about sports. They couldn't help but to see me as an athlete. It's like my size and physique were so abnormal to them that sports were all they could think about. These are the people who always come up to me and make jokes like, "How's the air up there?" or ask, "How tall are you?" with large eyes and their neck bent fully backward as if I'm as tall as a giraffe or something. I never understood these folks until I met a guy who was 7'6" … and I asked him the same question and did the same thing with my neck!

- **The true fans:** These are the people who will be my fans forever because they like me for who I am more than what I can do. The further I get away from my sports career, the more I love these people, because they still ask for my autograph and believe in whatever I am doing in my life and career. When I was a popular athlete, I got TIRED of people asking for my autograph. Now, I love it. It makes me feel special. And you're probably thinking, "But he said don't associate attention with value." You're right. I did. You see,

I, too, am still in process. Don't judge.

Understanding the reasons why people stopped contacting me and supporting me was so healing. In fact, I started to enjoy the freedom of going out to eat without getting interrupted. Many famous people can tell you that popularity has its perks, but it also has a price. That price is called normalcy. You can and will get use to a healthier, more normal dose of attention eventually.

Be patient with yourself

The faster you can accept the end of your career, the faster your mind and heart will heal from the grief that comes with the transition. This could take decades for some and minutes for others. Every athlete's process is different.

One factor that affects that timeline is the strength of the person's athletic identity, or the degree to which an individual identifies with the athlete role and looks to others for acknowledgement. The stronger an individual's athletic identity, the more challenging the process of acceptance may be, and the longer it may take. In other words, if you have little or no idea who you are or what you're gifted to do outside of sports—if your identity is solely defined by your role as an athlete—it may take you longer to accept your career is done.

Be patient during the process of letting go and redefining yourself. Don't compare your process to someone else's. I used to look at other former athletes and wonder how in the world they seemed so happy. I thought something was wrong with me because I seemed to be the only one depressed and struggling. But the truth is I wasn't alone. I just hadn't found other athletes in the same phase of transition. Many athletes in the world were experiencing similar issues, but they weren't talking about it. And then there were those who didn't have such a strong athletic identity. Several had parents who had helped them develop a more well-rounded identity. They had clearly defined ambitions and skills that weren't strictly connected to being an athlete. Although some may have played longer and achieved a higher level of success on the field, they didn't struggle as badly as I did. As you assess where you are in the process of accepting the end of your career in your heart, soul and mind, you may get frustrated that the desire to become or continue to be a professional athlete still tugs at you. You may be tempted to believe you'll never get rid of that longing. Believe me when I say that couldn't be further from the truth. You will get to a point where you're OK with your new, non-athlete status. Stop beating yourself up about how far you have to go, and start celebrating how far you've come. Continue to work through the rest of this book; the steps outlined here will help you.

Stages, not requirements

You may have heard of Swiss psychiatrist Elisabeth Kübler-Ross' five stages of grief[11]:

1. Denial

2. Anger

3. Bargaining

4. Depression

5. Acceptance

Some people think that in order to deal with death of any kind, including relationships and careers, you must follow those steps in sequential order. Many sources say Kübler-Ross regretted writing the phases in a way that implied a certain order. Her stages of grief are observations, most helpful if you find yourself stuck in one of them. However, you don't have to work through them chronologically to get to a place of acceptance. The five stages are common after a loss of something special, but they are not mandatory. You might skip right to acceptance if you apply the principles and strategies shared throughout this chapter. Acceptance and peace of mind will be yours when you're diligent about applying what you've learned.

Let's work out:

1. **Write down what your potential was**. Get it all out. Write down how good you could have been, how fast you could have run, how elite you could have become, everybody you were better than, etc. Read it out loud to a friend or family member. Don't suppress your feelings because you think you need to be tough. Isolation and hiding your feelings are not healthy. Find somebody you trust or email our team if you need to get your feelings off your chest.

2. **Write down your accomplishments—the potential you actually reached.** How good were you, really? What were your stats? What level did you play at? Etc.

3. **Accept your accomplishments. Let go of your potential.** It's OK to grieve. Don't suppress your feelings. See a counselor or psychiatrist if

you need to. I did. Write down what you will do to let go of your potential.

4. **Pay close attention to your daily conversations.** Watch for when you are talking about potential versus actual accomplishments.

5. **Make a commitment to no longer talk about potential.** Only talk about achievement, and even then be careful. There's a huge difference between talking about the past and dwelling in the past.

6. **Review the three symptoms of haters.** Honestly evaluate if you have any of these symptoms. Then, start celebrating others.

7. **Review the four types of fans: Bandwagoners, Businesspersons, Admirers, True fans.** Identify people who you may have placed in the wrong category. Practice Fan Forgiveness and move forward. Choose to thank and spend more time with your true fans.

8. **Review Elisabeth Kübler-Ross' five stages of grief.** Do you particularly identify with any of the stages? Allow yourself to feel the full weight of your emotions. Remember, they're stages, not requirements. Give yourself time to grieve, but don't delay your healing process because you feel like you have to walk through each stage.

9. **Write a goodbye letter to sports.** Celebrate the moments you've had together, and document what being an athlete has meant to your life in what I call a "Gratitude Letter to Sport." Leave all of your feelings on the page, and get ready

to move on. If you need an example, search YouTube for "Darryll Stinson, NCAA letter to sport," and you'll find my Gratitude Letter to Sport.

discovering your identity and purpose. The next step on The Athlete Transition Roadmap is to believe with full confidence that there's a satisfying career and life for you that are greater than your life as an athlete.

Too many athletes rush into a new career with an old mindset. They find a good paying job, yet they're not as passionate about work as they were about their sport. They may not be depressed, but they don't walk around with the same confidence and energy they once had. They've moved on, but they're embracing the unhealthy mentality that their current path is second best to their former life. They still walk around with a little bit of emptiness inside, subconsciously believing their best days are behind them. Now their only option is to work hard, try to enjoy life and retire at a decent age.

If you feel that way, let me encourage you with an important announcement. Your best days are in front of you not behind you. Your "glory days" will be nothing compared to your future days. There is a life and a career for you that is better than your life as an athlete.

The key word is better. The struggle at this stage is that it's going to **feel** like nothing out there is better than sports. You'll be tempted to think there's nothing as stimulating as training hard, competing harder, singing victory songs with your teammates, hearing the fans cheer and the band play, or sensing the anticipation and excitement during the national anthem. I'll admit, those thoughts have a degree of truth. There is nothing like sports. But there is something more fulfilling and more impactful. The challenge is for you to believe it.

Not believing that there was a better purpose or a life for me is one of the main reasons I couldn't quit football and put my body through so much torment to continue to play. To me, the pain of living without sports was greater than the physical pain of playing with

a severe injury. I knew I could be successful in other
career fields. I had a phenomenal work ethic. I was a
good salesperson and had the potential to be a good
writer and communicator. But I thought those career
paths were boring and unfulfilling. I didn't want to sit in
front of a computer and send emails all day. I didn't want
to be a sports anchor, and I surely didn't want to coach.
A lot of athletes love the game so much they're fulfilled
just being around sports. Not me. I didn't want to be
around the game. I wanted to be in the game. I wanted
to experience the immense pressure that comes when the
win is on the line. I wanted to feel the adrenaline rush
of a big play. I wanted to strut around with confidence
while wearing my jersey after a championship. Those
experiences are why I got up at 4 or 5 in the morning
and pushed myself to get better every day.

Although my unbelief in a brighter future led me on
a terrifying path of low self-esteem, my experience at
the psychiatric unit in Detroit led me to believe there
was … no, there had to be … a better life and career
for me. You'll read more about this later, in the chapter
"What Really Happened?"

In the meantime, if you're struggling to believe your
best days are ahead, here are a few tips that worked
for me.

1. Change your language.

The language you use on a daily basis describes the
mindset and beliefs you have about life This is why
it was dangerous as a player to always talk about your
last win because the greatest enemy of future success
is often past success. If you talk about your last win
too much instead of preparing for the next game, you
decrease your chances of winning. It works the same

way in life. Your athletic career was your last win. Now it's time to prepare for your next one.

The last chapter addressed the danger of continuously talking about your athletic career. There we dealt with the "why" that is inspiring those conversations. Now we'll focus on how to properly talk about your athletic experience. If you're conquering the lessons of the acceptance chapter and are no longer talking about your potential and instead are having healthier conversations about your achievements—great! However, those conversations still sabotage your future if you don't continue to improve the way you talk about your athletic career.

Your language doesn't just reveal your mindset, it shapes your beliefs. If you talk about your athletic career as if it were the "good ol' days," it always will be. The opposite is true, as well. If you talk about your future as if it will be the best days of your life, then it can and will.

Let me say that again: If you talk about your future as if it will be the best days of your life, then it can and will be.

It doesn't matter if you became a hall of famer or a legend as an athlete. I don't care if you're Michael Jordan or Danica Patrick. If you choose to believe your best days are ahead of you, then they will be. All you have to do is believe. Not hope. Not think. Not guess. **Believe.** Use your language to create your future. Declare powerful words on a daily basis!

Literally say out loud statements such as:

- My best days are ahead of me!
- My future life will be so much more fulfilling than my life as an athlete!
- I killed it as an athlete ... and I'm going to crush whatever is next!

- People may think they've seen the best of me, but they "ain't seen nothing yet"! There's much more of me for the world to see!
- I've got books to write, dreams to build, ideas to manifest and people to help! (Insert your own ideas here, even if they're just the tiniest thoughts of what may be possible.)

Your declaration will become your situation. The thoughts you think and the words you use on a daily basis will create the life you experience. Your belief in the future will increase, as you declare positive beliefs. You'll begin to experience in reality what you have been declaring with your voice and believing in your mind.

2. Find values worth living for that have nothing to do with your ego.

I was self-absorbed. Life was all about me throughout my athletic journey. Everything was about my success. My fame. My income. My records. I mean, yeah, I wanted to give back. I wanted to buy my mom a house and my dad that brand new Toyota Sequoia he wanted. But even my desire to give back was all about my ego. I wanted to be "The Man." Giving to others was just another form of selfishness because I wanted to be praised and adored for my generosity. I had the right intentions, but the wrong heart.

That changed once I took the spotlight off me. A new and genuine focus on others made it possible for my past to fuel my future instead of being a barrier to it. I realized sharing my life experiences with others could make their lives better. That passion to help others became a driving force that eventually demolished the roadblocks which had kept me from advancing into a meaningful, satisfying life. The chart below—let's call it Ego Eliminator 2.0—highlights a few areas where focusing on others accelerated my belief in the future.

Focus on me	Focus on others
I hated going to my team's football games because it hurt not to be on the field.	I started going to my team's football games to bring energy and wisdom to my teammates.
I avoided talking to and hanging around athletes because it reminded me that I wasn't one.	I engaged in conversations with athletes because I realized they needed people who cared about them as people—not just as athletes.
I never shared my struggles with addiction and suicide because I didn't want people to think less of me.	I started to share my story and began writing this book because it encouraged and inspired others.
I wanted to be a professional athlete so I could be adored.	I wanted to better the lives of other people so they could experience the abundant life.

The more my life became about helping others instead of boosting my ego, the more I wanted to live. I started to wake up excited about future opportunities. I started to dream of the way the world could be better with my help. And guess what else? I stopped missing sports so much and started making moves to better the lives of more and more people.

By focusing on others, I've been able to help thousands of people stop selling drugs, overcome depression,

stop attempting suicide, quit smoking weed, start businesses, repair relationships, gain confidence and pursue
their dreams. That's the power of the spotlight no longer
being on you!

3. Borrow others' belief in you.
Remember that sometimes you have to borrow someone
else's belief in you before you can believe in yourself.

How many times have you heard someone tell you
how good you were in sports? Didn't it make you feel
good and give you a greater sense of confidence? It works
the same way in life. Pay attention to the people who see
potential in you and love you enough to let you know.

This made a huge difference in my journey. I didn't
believe I had other talents. I wasn't the best with numbers. I hated being vocal and despised public speaking. I
nearly failed every science class, and I was only average
at every subject. I was confident in my ability to perform
well on the field but highly insecure about my ability
to succeed at a high level in any other career path. This
all changed after I met Pastor Travis Hall. A friend and
teammate of mine had started to attend this church in a
small storefront in Mount Pleasant, Michigan, after our
team chaplain, Trooper Mike White, invited him. My
friend kept telling my roommates and me we should visit
the church, but we definitely weren't the church type.

One day, though, we woke up on Sunday, smoked
our usual wake-and-bake blunt, and for some strange
reason one of us said, "Ya'll want to go to church today?"
We all said yes, got dressed and went to church ... high!
I'm pretty sure we smelled like weed and our eyes were
red, but nobody seemed to notice or care. It seemed
like they were just happy to welcome visitors seeing
as how there were seemingly only six or seven regular
attenders. I don't remember much of what the pastor

was preaching. I do, however, vividly recall the way he was preaching like he was in a big auditorium—even though we were in a small storefront. He was really passionate about whatever he was talking about. I even checked over my shoulder a few times to see if he was seeing people in the room that I wasn't. At the end of his message, he asked if anyone wanted to receive prayer … and we all stood up and walked forward. We figured that since we were the only new people there, he must have been talking to us.

Funny thing though—when he came toward me, instead of praying like he did for my teammates, he started to talk. He placed his hand on my shoulder, looked me in the eye, and started telling me he believed in me and could see me doing all these amazing things. I remember thinking, "You don't even know me! Pastors are always just saying the same old stuff."

As time progressed, I came to learn I was half wrong. He didn't know me, and his words did sound cliché, but he did see something in me that I didn't and couldn't see in myself. He began to take me out to lunch to learn more about me. I went mainly because he paid, and the free food was an awesome way to satisfy the munchies I got from smoking. He would end just about every conversation by mentioning how he was proud of me and saw so much potential in me. I brushed it off each time. But after my sports career ended, I remembered his words and those conversations. I started to believe there was more to me than my athletic ability because he saw something great in me, and he had never even seen me play. I borrowed his belief in me until it became my own belief.

You can do that, too. Talk to a family member, coach, teammate or teacher. Ask them what gifts or skills they see in you beyond athletic talent. You might be afraid to have that conversation because you don't see much value in yourself other than your athleticism. Maybe you're like I was, confident in your ability to play sports but not in your ability to do anything else at a high level. Do me a favor. Borrow my belief in you.

Maybe you're thinking, "Why would I do that? You don't know me." You're right. I don't.

But my guess is that as an athlete, you had people cheer for you—which means you have influence. You no doubt made some tough decisions in high-pressure situations—which means you're decisive and a leader. You probably had to work hard despite physical pain or difficulties in life—which shows you have grit. You most certainly had to handle constructive criticism—which shows you're teachable. You had to work as a team—which means you can work well with others in any situation.

Those qualities alone are enough for me to believe in you. And it doesn't begin to describe whatever else is buried inside of your heart that you'll learn to uncover in the next chapter. So, if you don't have someone in your life who sees gifts and values your uniqueness, borrow my belief in you. There's so much more for you in your future than there has been in your past. You have yet to experience the fullness life has to offer and the impact you will make.

4. Use others' success as hope for you.
You've heard, "If they can do it, so can you? Monkey see, monkey do?" They're cheesy and cliché, but true. In order to believe in a promising future, you have to know you're not alone. Every year, millions of athletes will transition out of sports. Some will do so successfully and in a healthy manner. Some will not. Either way, you're not alone.

I thought I was the only one who struggled with my transition, which intensified my depression. It made me feel terrible about myself. I remember looking at others who had left sports, and they all seemed happy like they were having the time of their life. And there I was depressed, swallowing pills, smoking weed and drinking alcohol. I wondered what was so wrong with me that I was having such a hard time? As I started to talk to others though, I found more people who were going through similar transition challenges. I also discovered that what people post on social media is their highlight reel and often not an accurate picture of their real life. I had to stop comparing the raw film of my life to their social media highlights.

When I first launched Second Chance Athletes in 2017, I shared my story about the challenges I had after sports and how they led me to attempt suicide. I was shocked by the number of responses I received from athletes who were experiencing the same struggles and thought they were the only one! One woman said she broke down crying while she was at work. Another guy said he was stuck in life and hadn't realized it was because his heart was still stuck to sports. People I played against in elementary school and people who were twice my age responded to my story. They played different sports, had different stories and faced different challenges. Yet, they had at least one thing in common—they thought they were alone. **You are not alone!** Other people are facing and overcoming the transition challenges … and so will you.

Remember how you would watch films of your competitors and know you could beat them? Or watch other athletes perform and get excited because you knew you could do what they did, only better? Same principle applies here. You'll find stories on our website of other

athletes who have made it through the transition challenges. They have families, own businesses, travel the
world, write books, run companies and love life.

Consider their success—not as a pointer to what you
don't have—but as a promise that you can do it, too.
Use their successes as hope for you.

You might find it hard to believe right now, but
I assure you that if you focus on the possibilities of
the future, it will help you get over sports and move
forward with your life. The next chapter will help you
more with that.

Let's work out:

1. **Tell someone about your favorite sports
   moments.** Tell someone else about your current job or life. Compare your excitement in
   talking about your athletic career with your
   passion for your current job.

2. **Shift your passion from your past to your
   present**. Believe that your best days are ahead.
   For the next 14 days, tally each time you talk
   about the past versus each time you talk about
   the present. Begin reminding yourself multiple times a day that your best days are in your
   future and not your past.

3. **Find and write positive declarations about
   your future.** Post them in visible places as
   reminders to yourself.

4. **Jot down anything outside of you that makes
   you feel valuable** (friends, fans, trophies, med-
   als, social media followers, etc.). Replace those
   external things with internal qualities that you

like about yourself. Remind yourself often that your value is determined by who you choose to be on the inside—not by people or things outside of your control.

5. **Make a list of core values that are important to you**. Begin to live your life based on these values instead of ego.

6. **Borrow others' belief in you.** Ask people around you to describe their favorite qualities in you. Ask them to list your top three strengths. Enjoy the ah-ha moments!

7. **Find and follow other athletes who have transitioned successfully.** Use their story as hope for you.

CHAPTER 5
DISCOVER YOUR PURPOSE

The big questions:

1. What is my purpose?
2. What career path is best for me?
3. How do I describe my purpose when I have multiple passions and talents?

The goal:

To go through the third step of The Athlete Transition Roadmap to know your life's purpose and gain clarity about your dreams and career.

It's been said often and credited to many: "The two most important days in your life are the day you are born and the day you discover why."[12]

Do you play sports?

After I retired, the first time someone asked how tall I was and whether I played sports, my heart ached, and I swear it stopped beating for a few seconds. For the first time in my life, my answer was, "No … I don't… play any sports." I could barely get the words out. It felt unnatural to say that, and it came with a surge of discouragement. Like many others around the world, I had played sports since I was a child. I couldn't recall a time when my answer was no to someone who asked me if I played sports.

The harder question to answer now was, "If I'm no longer an athlete … then who am I?"

I started researching everything I could find about discovering your life's purpose. I bought online courses, went to events and read numerous books. I read dissertations and articles and watched every YouTube video I could find about purpose, meaning, calling or whatever you want to name the ultimate driving force in life. Much of what I found was the same advice presented in different ways. Many life coaches, educators, philosophers, pastors, thought leaders, etc., advise you to compose a list of things you're passionate about so you can select the one you're most passionate about and, voila, you found your purpose.

Many of them taught the same principles, such as:

- "Your purpose is to be a blessing to others."
- "Your purpose is to help other people discover their purpose."
- "Your purpose is to be the best person you can be to the people you love."

My mentor used to tell me that where your gifts meet your passion, you'll find your purpose. Those narratives are wise, and I say them from time to time when I speak to a group. Yet, for me, football and basketball were my passions! Running fast, jumping high and making plays were my gifts! So, what do you do when sports are your passion, but you can no longer play? What do you do when your talent is your athleticism, but you're no longer an athlete? **What do you do when what you love to do is not an option?**

The best advice I received in this phase of my journey came from my mentor, Travis Hall. You heard about him in the last chapter. He's passionate about helping people discover and walk in their purpose, and he helped me discover mine. He gave me a series of self-discovery questions that I've listed here for you. They're also available for free on his website, www.cultivatemypurpose.com

1. What in life bothers you the most?

2. What would you do with your life if you knew you couldn't fail?

3. What would you do with your life if you knew your family would support your dream unconditionally?

4. What would you do with your life if you knew money wasn't an issue?

5. What in life are you naturally passionate about?

6. What comes easy for you that doesn't come as easy for your friends or family?

7. If you had 10 extra hours a week to spend on anything you wanted, how would you spend them?

8. What are you willing to sacrifice for?

9. Who are the people you're naturally drawn to and want to emulate?

10. How have the struggles that you and your family endured impacted your life?

11. What would you do with your life if you knew you wouldn't have to face the pain of dealing with your past?

Hall provides a description for each question on his website that can help you work through your answers.

A summary of what I came up with when I spent time exploring them:

- Speaking (I wrote it down even though I was insecure about my speaking ability)
- Writing
- Ideation
- Coaching
- Relationships
- Business
- Leadership
- Rapping (admittedly, this one was a stretch, lol)

That's a pretty solid list, but, unfortunately, I didn't love any of those things as much as I loved sports. My research on purpose drove me deeper into depression because every time I found a new video or article, my hopes would rise, and I'd think, "This resource is finally going to provide me with the clarity I've been seeking." But things never got more clear. I just became more confused. I spent months exploring new interests. I tried to write an album, build a speaking career and network, but I still couldn't find anything I loved as much as being an athlete.

Then one day, I suddenly had a liberating thought. What if none of my passions were fulfilling because I wasn't as good at them as I was at sports?

As an athlete, I set records. I hit game-winners. I could compete with the best. When it came to writing, I thought I was below average. Coaching—average. Rapping—I had bars. Just kidding … I was average. Business … a beginner. Speaking … insecure. Leadership … indecisive. Every non-athletic skill I had was average at best. None of those skills was going to get me in the newspaper or on national television. None of them was going to entice people to line up and ask for my autograph. None of them was going to give me the adrenaline rush dominating my opponents gave me. I simply wasn't exceptional or elite at any of my nonathletic skills.

This discovery was pivotal in my process of transitioning. It helped me realize that just because I *didn't* love anything more than sports, didn't mean I *couldn't* love anything more than sports. I correctly figured if I increased my competency, I would increase my passion. Let's take public speaking. It occurred to me that if I worked hard at speaking like I did with sports, if I put the hours in, got better every day and became exceptional at it, at some point I could grow to love it! Think about it. Most people don't love to do things they're terrible at, but almost everyone loves to do things they're great at.

Increased competency + practice = increased passion

I actually hated speaking in front of people. Have you ever participated in a conversational icebreaker? I hated those! My throat would get tight knowing I would have to stand up, say my name and tell people one thing they didn't know about me. When I finally spoke, I would mumble so people couldn't hear me very well because I hated the sound of my voice.

Former All-American football player Brian Pruitt[13] was one of the first to invite me to speak in public. He asked me to talk with the young men at Power of Dad, his non-profit organization that focuses on helping fatherless children. I was so nervous and insecure that I wrote out my entire speech and recorded myself reading it out loud with an app on my phone. When it came time to speak, I put my phone in my pocket, strung the headphones underneath my hoodie and put one earbud in so it would look like I just forgot to take an earbud out. Then I hit play on the app and proceeded to give the speech by repeating word for word what was on the recording. The problem was that I didn't record it as if I were speaking it live. I was just reading what I wrote, so the pace and rhythm were much different. I ended up speaking a lot faster than the recording. It was awful. I got off sync and started repeating sentences multiple times and saying things that didn't even make sense. I'm still embarrassed thinking about it! People who hear me speak now don't believe me when I tell them that story.

I've clipped together a video of one of the first times I shared my story in public. Much like my Power of Dad engagement, I did a horrible job. I didn't try to repeat after a recording though. It was just all me and all bad. The speech made absolutely no sense because I didn't know how to organize my thoughts to communicate clearly. I mumbled the entire time and barely made eye contact with the audience. You can go to my YouTube page to watch the video if want.

Yet, while I was bad at speaking and hated it with everything in me, I knew it was something I could do to help other people. I trusted that if I learned more about the art and mechanics of speaking and spent hours practicing, I would grow to love it more. I retook an undergraduate public speaking course. I volunteered as an assistant teacher for a public speaking class at Central Michigan University. I shared my story with athletic teams. I treated every conversation with someone like it was a speech. I researched speaking techniques and best practices. I joined a local Toastmasters Club. I recorded and critiqued myself. Over time, I did get better! And the better I got, the more comfortable I became. The more comfortable I became, the better I spoke. The better I spoke, the more engaging I became. The more engaging I became, the more I liked public speaking. Now pay attention: Today I speak to audiences all the time. And the pre-speech adrenaline rush I get knowing what I have to say has the power and potential to change lives is comparable to what I used to experience in sports.

The same thing can happen for you. There is something in your life that you know deep down you're supposed to be doing. Maybe like me with speaking, you dismiss it because you don't like doing it and aren't great at it yet. I'm not suggesting your purpose in life is to do something you don't like. I think you should love what you do. I'm suggesting that you owe it to yourself and the people you will impact to examine why you don't like doing certain things. Is it because you're not awesome at them? Is it because you're afraid to fail?

Sometimes fear and insecurity keep you from discovering your purpose. That's what I was doing with speaking. I knew one of the reasons I survived suicide was so I could share my story and help others climb out of that dark hole of depression. Yet, because I was insecure about my speaking abilities, I told myself I hated public speaking. It was a good excuse. And there was some truth to it. I did hate public speaking. I hated the process of gathering my thoughts. I hated trying to come up with memorable statements so people would retain my messages. I hated worrying about my clothes and if they were messed up or appropriate. That was only half of the truth, though. The other half was that I knew I was meant to do it. That's the part I never told anyone because if I did, they would ask or encourage me to speak. The pain of pretending like I wasn't supposed to be a speaker was easier to bear than the pain of getting in front of people and failing.

I was afraid to fail because I had gotten used to being elite. When I failed at something as an athlete, it was easy for me to correct. If I missed a tackle, I could correct that error in a week or sometimes even the next play. If I needed to get stronger, I could do so in a couple of months. Because when you've reach elite status in any industry or with any skill, adjustments tend to be minor and require less time, energy and effort.

I had forgotten what it was like to be a beginner and start from scratch. I had been so good at sports for so long that not being good at something was awkward. Ask me to do anything athletic, and I would pick up on it quickly. Even though my main sports were basketball and football, I also was good at track in high school. I was good at nearly anything athletic, including bowling, lifting, golf, softball, volleyball, tennis—you name it. I'm sure you were, too. Athleticism often is transferable across many sports. And although I was a hard worker, admittedly, I was naturally athletic. It runs in my family. My father played D1 football and was a beast. My first cousin got a scholarship to run track at a D1 school. My aunt Barbara Stinson qualified for the '86 Olympics and at the time of this writing is still ranked nationally for her 400-meter dash. Not to mention the dozen other family members who would have been great athletes if they had stayed out of trouble.

Since athleticism was natural to me, I had a habit of quitting things that didn't come easy to me. I'll talk more about that later in this chapter, but not being a naturally good speaker, I would avoid considering public speaking as a career choice.

Your purpose beyond sports may be something you are not that great at in the beginning. You may just be decent at writing, working with computers, organizing projects, woodworking or understanding the human body. Don't dismiss a potential talent that may be your true purpose just because it doesn't come natural to you. Don't talk yourself out of what may be your purpose just because you're insecure about starting at the beginning of mastery again. Thoroughly examine your "beginner" talents and internal desires to make sure you are processing what could be the greatest gift to you and to others. If you're unsure, just try it out. Start reading books, listening to podcasts and studying others. Start practicing that skill or shadow someone who's doing what you think you may be meant to do. Imagine yourself being awesome at that career. If you like the feeling of being awesome at it, maybe it's a clue you're supposed to develop that gift. This will take time, but it's worth exploring. Without this principle, I would still be telling myself I hate motivational speaking instead of impacting the world with my voice.

Your purpose is bigger than your career

I had a greater understanding of my purpose once I
started public speaking. The better I got at it and the
more opportunities came my way, the more fulfillment
I got from doing it. I knew it was something I was
meant to do, and I finally was doing it with success.
Yet, I knew there was more I needed to do to find my
unique purpose. There were more desires and talents
inside of me.

Maybe you're feeling the same way. Maybe you're
doing something you enjoy, but you know there's more
inside you. Maybe doing well in your career, yet you
still sense there's something greater for you to accomplish—something big, innovative ... even revolutionary.
You can't quite put your finger on it. It's hard to put
it into words. But deep down, you know there's more.
And you're right. You see, purpose is bigger than career.

Some ways to discover the "more"

Discover the why behind your whats. Your career is
what you do. It's your job title and description. Many
people make the mistake of thinking their purpose is
what they do. If you were to ask them their purpose in
life, they would say it's to be a teacher, writer, artist or
lawmaker. Most times, they love what they do and gain
fulfillment from it, but sometimes, deep down, they
know there's even more to their life than what they
do. Some try to fix this internal longing for more by
switching careers, only to be happy for another three
to five years and then switch again. Some simply settle
into a career and wait for retirement perks. And there's
nothing wrong with enjoying a satisfying career with
retirement perks as long as it fulfills you to the max.

But for those who are not completely fulfilled in their life and career and have a desire to do something more, this chapter will help you

Imagine the power of discovering the why behind what you do. Especially because what you do may change throughout your life, but your why will most likely remain the same. You may go from sales to working with children. Or from working in one department to managing another. Careers change, but purpose rarely does.

For instance, I'm passionate about and called to write. That's my what. And my why is to help misfits turn their pain into purpose and profit so they can experience abundance in all areas of their lives. I do that primarily through writing and speaking. See the difference? Knowing my why frees me from the prison of thinking my purpose is one-dimensional. Knowing my why frees me to operate in my calling in diverse ways. I can help others experience abundance through speaking, writing, rap, financial education, entrepreneurship, coaching, etc.

When I learned this tip to discovering my purpose, it pushed me to dig deep and find the core of my passions. Think of it this way: We think if we're passionate about helping children, we'll find a job working with kids, and we'll be fulfilling our purpose. But daycare workers, little league coaches and juvenile social workers all work with kids for different reasons. Their whys are all different. Discovering your why will give you more clarity in your life's purpose. It will help you be more versatile. And, interestingly, it potentially helps you establish more streams of income.

Focus on others

Another tip for discovering purpose is to ask, "What am I trying to make happen for others?"

Consider a woman who's a youth basketball coach. That's her passion. That's her what. Yet, she feels like there's more, so she seeks to understand her why— and that is to give kids something to do to stay out of trouble because boredom pushed her to do a lot of bad things when she was young. Now she knows her what and her why. But she still feels a lack of clarity in her life's purpose.

Then she asks herself what she's trying to make happen for the children—what she's trying to accomplish by helping them. At that point, she discovers that deep down she's trying to eliminate obstacles that keep children from reaching their full potential. This explains her love of coaching and the energy she feels volunteering at the local pregnancy prevention agency. It's her why.

Imagine how liberating that discovery would be. She could be a coach for 20 years and hit a mid-life crisis, confused about what to do with the rest of her life. If she didn't know her purpose, she could get depressed or discouraged and feel like she wasted 20 years of her life. Or she could start working for the government, fighting against poverty, and find out she loves government work more than coaching. She would realize that fighting poverty and coaching are both ways she operated in her purpose to eliminate obstacles that prevented youth from reaching their full potential. Now her whole life makes sense.

By the way, today I know that even as an athlete my why was always a driving force. I loved to see families making memories while attending a game. I loved seeing packed arenas and businesses and vendors making money. I loved when my teammates made unbelievable plays. Today, I understand that, by playing sports, I was helping all of them tap into the abundance of love, joy and happiness available to us all.

Be encouraged that although transitioning out of sports is tough, you haven't wasted your life! You're just changing your what as you gain clarity about your why.

Find your common denominator

I once had a conversation with a talented young woman who was wrestling with discovering her purpose. All she knew is that she liked working with pets, and she liked helping young girls. I asked what she liked about those activities. She liked working with pets because they are cute and lovable, and she liked working with girls to help them see that they spent too much time chasing love from guys rather than from God.

She elaborated and said it broke her heart to see young women wasting years of their lives trying to get love from a guy who gave them none in return. Normally, I would keep asking why and "what she was trying to make happen for others" until we found something deeper that resonated with her. But I noticed a common denominator in her interests ... love.

I mentioned that the word "love" connected her two interests; it seemed like she wanted the young girls and the pets to be and feel loved. And since she was a Christian, I said more specifically, it seems like it bothers her when people are not experiencing Jesus' love for them. Perhaps she was trying to help them experience the fullness of God's love? Perhaps her purpose is to bring the love of Christ to the lives of people and, in her case, pets too? She paused, thought about it, and her face lit up.

"That's it!" she said. "It all makes sense now!" The next week at her young adults' small group she immediately started operating in her purpose with a higher level of clarity and confidence. She gave a message about

God's love that helped her entire group experience His love for them—some for the very first time. When you discover your purpose, you get more effective at everything you do. It's like a screwdriver that's been hammering nails all its life and finally discovers it was meant to work with screws. When she told me about her message, she was "on 10!" a phrase my friends and I use to describe people at peak levels of energy, excitement and fulfillment.

This is what happens when you get beyond the surface and access the depths of your mind and heart. This is what you'll get to experience through this discovery process.

Your purpose is to change the world

Sound a little extreme? I know. Not everyone will become a Martin Luther King Jr., Abraham Lincoln, Steve Jobs, or Orville or Wilbur Wright. But try asking yourself questions such as: "If I could create the perfect world, what would it be like?" "How would people treat each other?" "How would people learn?" "What technologies would exist?" "What would the condition of the environment be?" Be as descriptive as possible in your questions and in your answers.

Pay attention to what excites you most. Your excitement often is a destiny clue. You find energy in what you envision because your purpose is to help create that world.

Questions like those helped confirm my why. I imagined a world where people were full of joy and never had to worry about money, food or other basic needs. The world I pictured was full of people who knew their purpose and were actively engaged in creating the world they envisioned. And dreaming of this world made me want to take off running and jumping with joy. It was a world of abundance, not scarcity. It was a world where everyone was alive, happy and equipped to do what they loved. It was a world where everyone sacrificed for the good of others. A world where acceptance, not judgment, was the norm. A world where love was freely given and not just to people who look and think the same. A world void of murder, jealousy, envy, hatred, arrogance, pride, crimes and all evil in general. This was the world I was called to help create!

Sound unrealistic? Maybe. But that didn't stop Ghandi, Alan Shepard, Mark Zuckerberg, Billy Graham, Nelson Mandela and Bill Gates. They didn't pull back, so why should we?

Imagine the world you long to live in, and it will help you discover the purpose for which you are alive.

Final thoughts on discovery

Discovering your purpose isn't a luxury reserved for only some people. It's available to everyone, and it's mandatory to reaching your full potential in life after sports. Full satisfaction is possible only when you have a clear understanding of your purpose. Going beyond surface-level questions and digging deep to find your why can be hard. Some of my clients love reflecting, journaling and thinking about this type of stuff. Others can't stand the abstract. They hate thinking about their past. They hate navigating the depths of their soul. Some want to treat purpose discovery like a box on their task list to be checked off in 15 minutes. But it doesn't work that way. Clarity costs. It cost me hundreds of hours of research, years of trial and error, days of frustration and disappointment, and countless moments of wanting to quit. Yet the pain I had to endure in the process of discovering my purpose was so worth the life I get to live and the people I have the opportunity to impact.

Nothing in life will energize you like operating in your purpose. Knowing your purpose will open unimaginable opportunities for you. It will help you fall in love with your life and out of lust with your athletic career. You must—and you will—discover your purpose so that you can walk in the fullest expression of yourself.

The world deserves all of you.

Let's go to work:

1. **Write down a list of skills, interests and passions.**

2. **Work through Travis Hall's 11 purpose discovery questions.**

3. **Spend time journaling and reflecting on the following questions:**

   - What is your why?
   - What are you trying to make happen for others?
   - What are you trying to accomplish through your work?
   - What are the similarities between your interests?
   - What perfect world do you envision?

4. **Write out a 1-2 sentence purpose statement that describes what you believe to be your life's purpose based upon your observations from the first three exercises.** Example: My purpose is to help misfits turn their pain into

purpose and profit so that they can experience abundance in all areas of their life.

5. **Choose one or two skills for which you want to increase your competency.** Begin to study and practice that skill to see if you want to pursue a career in that area.

CHAPTER 6
PURSUE YOUR DREAMS LIKE A CHAMPION

The big questions:

1. How do I achieve my dreams?

2. How do I become highly successful in my industry?

3. Why does my career beyond sports seem so difficult?

The goal:

To go through the hard work of step four of The Athlete Transition Roadmap and create and execute your game plan for achieving your career goals.

It wasn't enough for me to love my life like I loved it as an athlete. I wanted to be highly successful—an elite player in my career just like I was in sports. I'm not suggesting every former athlete feels this way, and it's OK if you don't. While this chapter will help all who read it, it's written specifically for those who desire to outperform peers and dominate the competition—for those who can't tolerate average in any area of life.

In Chapter 5 you discovered your purpose or gained some clarity. Now it's time to go after your dreams— elite style.

My favorite definition of pursue in Merriam-Webster's dictionary is "to find or employ measures to obtain or accomplish."[14] Pursuit is not aimless. It's strategic. It's intentional. It requires deep thought, wise counsel, sacrifice and commitment.

The quickest, most helpful advice I have for you in this step is to filter every life decision through the lens of your purpose. Never settle for less in pursuit of your purpose. I used to think the main reason people didn't pursue their purpose and chase their dreams was that they were confused and needed clarity. That's true for some. However, the longer I've done life coaching, the more I realize that usually isn't the case. A lot of people have a pretty good idea of what their life purpose is, they're just afraid to do what it takes to pursue it. They blame their finances or circumstances when, in reality, they're just afraid. Afraid of failing. Afraid of what people will think. Afraid of having to sacrifice their comfort or security in the short-term to build a more meaningful life.

It's been said that people only change when the fear of staying the same becomes greater than the fear of change. Too often, we overestimate the cost we'll pay to achieve our dreams and underestimate the benefits. We complain about how much money it will cost or time it will take to go back to school. We dread the process of obtaining 501c3 status or applying for a grant. We talk about how much money we'll need to launch a business. We focus so much on the challenges that we lose sight of the benefits.

Pursuing your purpose will require sacrifice

Fact: Pursuing your purpose will require sacrifice. But don't miss an opportunity to chase your dreams because the opportunity looks like a step down instead of a step up. In my research, I've discovered that often the larger platform a person will have, the greater the sacrifice will be. You have to give up to go up. Preparation precedes elevation. You have to go through something to get to something. You're going to fail, but failure is never final when you learn from it. I don't want this to discourage you. I want it to prepare you.

Think of when you faced a top opponent in sports. You watched film and saw them knock someone out in seconds, or you saw the person you're defending score 40 points on the best team in your league. Did watching your top-rated opponent cause you to train harder? I assume so. Why? Because you knew who you had to face. It's the same way with your dreams. Pursuing your purpose is like going after that top-rated opponent. It will require you to work harder, study longer and think smarter. It is not going to be easy! But I promise the process will be worth it. I guarantee the lives you're going to impact will be worth every early morning, every late night, every tear and every moment you felt like quitting.

I made sacrifices to pursue my purpose even when I was just starting out in my career after sports. In retrospect, I realize how every work experience prepared me for the next. Often, when clients get to this phase of transition, they are fed up with their current job, and now that they are clear about their purpose, they don't want to wait another day to experience their dreams. Sometimes regret settles in and they feel like they wasted so much time. Some lose patience with their boss, coworkers and work culture in general. Its kind of feels like last semester senior year in high school when you're just tired of high school and ready for college. Don't get discouraged if this is you. This chapter will help you start taking more intentional and strategic steps in the right direction but nothing you have been through will be wasted. Every past season of your life has prepared you for the one you are stepping into now. You may be making a complete career change or just a slight adjustment or expansion. No matter your situation, stay encouraged, trust your gut and just make the next right move.

My senior year in college was critical because I had to build a professional portfolio that had nothing to do with athletics in just two semesters—really one if you consider the time it takes to graduate and secure employment. Until senior year, I slacked horribly in school because there was no point in taking exams that wouldn't impact an NFL contract. I cheated and charmed my way through classes to stay eligible to play. Yet, despite having not applied myself much, I managed to land a paid public relations internship at CMU's University Communications. This great internship, combined with some volunteering and a part-time fundraising job with CMU's Alumni Relations team, gave me enough experience to become competitive in the workforce. Approaching graduation, I had job offers in Michigan, Georgia and Florida. I was proud. I had worked hard to build my resume and improve my communication skills, and it had paid off. I had good-paying career options prior to graduation!

Everything was fine until I had an unsettled feeling and an inner voice telling me something wasn't right. None of the jobs aligned with my desire to impact others through motivational speaking, life coaching and fostering community. After prayer, counsel and much thought, I decided to stay in Mount Pleasant to serve the visionary Travis Hall; I had a gut feeling my purpose was connected to his leadership. That may sound like no big deal, but I didn't have any job offers in or near Mount Pleasant. Travis' organization was not in a position to hire me. University Communications couldn't hire me because their only opening required at least three years of experience. I couldn't even find other paid internships in the area.

I had to make a choice. Should I accept a job offer far away from Mount Pleasant, or sacrifice all of them and stay to pursue what was in my heart? I decided to stay. I didn't know how I would pay my rent, fuel, utilities, cell phone bill or start working toward my financial goals, but I made up my mind I would rather follow my heart and fail than follow comfort and possibly miss the opportunity to fulfill my destiny.

I'd like to tell you that as soon as I decided to stay, the phone rang with a job opportunity. That didn't happen. Days passed ... then weeks. I applied to jobs that I was overqualified for and still wasn't hired. I was embarrassed to tell people I was jobless. When the subject came up, I ignored it. I thought closed doors were a sign I was headed in the wrong direction. Now I know that when you're pursuing your purpose, every closed door means you're one step closer to an open door.

The cheapest apartment I could find was a five-bedroom where I would stay with four people

I had never met. Family members and friends said I was stupid for staying in Mount Pleasant. They said it's cool to follow your gut, but you have to use your head. I wasn't mad that they doubted me because I was struggling with doubt, too. I had to make up my mind every day, sometimes multiple times a day, that I was doing the right thing. I shoveled snow with my bad back to make money. I served food at the local soup kitchen and saved the leftovers to cover my meals. I earned $20 to $40 a week mentoring troubled youth. I asked family members for money to cover expenses that I couldn't hustle enough to pay on my own. This went on for about six months, while I was volunteering for Big Brothers Big Sisters, the Isabella County Soup Kitchen and serving as an unpaid janitor at my church.

Then one day I received a call from CMU that University Communications had a position I should consider. I applied and got hired after my second interview. During that time, I also was asked to join the leadership team at my church as volunteer. Instantly, I went from being SUPER broke to having a full-time job with benefits and insurance and major responsibilities. I suddenly went from unpaid church janitor to church leader. It was an amazing feeling. I get emotional writing about it because I wanted to give up so many times and accept one of my out-of-town job offers. I cried so many nights wondering if I would end up homeless because I took a chance on fulfilling my dreams.

The sacrifice paid off. None of that would have happened if I had chosen convenience and "logic" instead of pursuing what seemed impossible. I could have just accepted a job elsewhere, but I had to sacrifice a good job for a great calling. I learned that your purpose is pricey, and it does not go on sale. You have to pay the cost. You have to do the work. You have to be willing to take scary risks. It's been said that in order to go where others wish they could go, you have to do what others aren't willing to do.

I see too many people give up on the pursuit of their purpose because they don't want to pay the price to get to the next level of their impact and destiny. I know writers who never become authors because overcoming writer's block was too hard. I know speakers who quit because they bombed their first speaking gig. I know entrepreneurs who settled for a 9-to-5 job that drains them because they didn't want to live in poverty while building their business. They wanted to chase their dreams, but they settled for less because they wouldn't sacrifice their comfort. As a result, comfort became a prison that held their dreams captive. They didn't realize the cost of admission to their destiny was sacrifice.

Let me ask: What would you do with your life if you didn't have to sacrifice time, money or your reputation to do it? What would you do if you could skip preparation and get straight to destination?

Consider the answers, then make up your mind now that you will not allow fear or sacrifice to keep you from what you really want and are intended to do.

Start where you are, with what you have, no matter how small

To pursue your purpose, you have to figure out how to start where you are, with what you have, no matter how small. If you're called to start a business but don't have the capital, raise or save the money. If you're called to write but have young kids, write for 15 minutes each night after they go to bed. If you're called to be a radio personality but can't get a job or internship, job shadow somebody or record yourself on your phone as if you were on-air. If you're called to speak but don't know where to start or how to get paid, research, do some free gigs or practice speaking in the mirror.

The best way to move forward is to learn the art of using what you have and where you are as transportation to the next step of your journey. You already have what you need to make it to your next step. It probably won't drop you at your destination, but it's enough to move you further on the journey.

Don't underestimate how quickly you can go from something seemingly small and insignificant to large and impactful, especially in a world where social media gives everyone a free platform. Instantly, I went from an unpaid church janitor to church leader after six months of feeling small and insignificant. Again, there's nothing wrong with being a janitor. If that's your calling—awesome. You, your work and your impact matter. But for me, unpaid janitorial work was tough knowing that I had a desire to pursue a much different career path. My willingness to do what felt like small things well, with the right attitude is what led to my next big break. The same can be true for you. If you're faithful with small opportunities, you'll find larger ones that are more in alignment with your purpose and dreams. One of my favorite quotes is, "He who is too big for small things is too small for big things."[15] Success happens when preparation meets opportunity. Keep doing the best you can with what you have and be watching for bigger opportunities to come your way.

From small rags to big riches

Sylvester Stallone was born July 6, 1946, in New York City.[16] Despite having paralysis in parts of his face and slurred speech due to birth complications, and despite his parents divorcing when he was 9, Stallone dreamed of being an actor. He attended school in Philadelphia, where he started acting and became a football star. Later, he enrolled at the University of Miami to study drama and started writing screenplays. Stallone dropped out of college to pursue an acting career and ran into extremely hard times. A variety of small acting roles in television and movies only left him homeless.

Yet Stallone kept taking small steps toward his destiny and continued to write while searching for acting gigs. One day, he got a spur of inspiration and spent 20 straight hours finishing writing "Rocky," a sports drama film featuring Rocky Balboa's journey from being an uneducated debt collector to the heavyweight champion of the world.

Stallone, hoping to star as Rocky, pitched his script to producers. They loved the script, but they didn't want a no-name actor. Their plan was to cast big actors of the time, such as Robert Redford or Burt Reynolds, to play Balboa. Producers offered him $350,000 for rights to the script, but Stallone refused, even though he only had $100 left in the bank. After much negotiation and a substantial budget cut, producers agreed in 1976 to let Stallone star in his own film.

The rest of his story has made history. The "Rocky" series has brought in more than a billion dollars worldwide. Stallone gained a worldwide reputation as actor, writer and director. He also is an accomplished artist, with paintings and sculptures in respected exhibitions at Art Basil, The Russian State Museum and the Nice Museum of Contemporary Art in France.

Stallone's story is one of many such accounts of men and women who have had huge opportunities after making big sacrifices and being faithful with small opportunities. You don't need a great platform to become great. You don't need to be in a big city to make a difference. Greatness is proven through one's ability to do small things ... well and consistently.

Pursuing your purpose will require sacrifices. You'll have to start small and use what you have where you are. Every book ever written started with one word. Every multi-million-dollar business deal started with an introduction. Great achievement really does come from small beginnings. It doesn't matter how busy you are or how much money you don't have. We all have the same time and could use more money. The hard truth is that many people in this world have done more than we have with less than what we have. The success of your pursuit of purpose is determined by your willingness to sacrifice and treat small opportunities like big ones. Are you willing to sacrifice what's average to pursue what's great? Are you willing to sacrifice comfort to reach destiny? Are you willing to treat small opportunities like once-in-a-lifetime opportunities?

The effort myth

There's a myth among athletes that it's possible to give more than 100 percent. Yet, there is no such thing as 150 percent effort. There's only 100 percent effort; 100 is the maximum. Often when I coach people, they struggle with learning the new habit of consistency. They wake up without intentional time scheduled to work on their purpose, and they move toward their goals without accountability. Usually, they go through ups and downs, hot and cold days. One day they wake up and give it only 75 percent of their effort. Then they think they'll make up for it the next day and go extra hard! "I'll pull an all-nighter! I'll give it 125 percent." What they don't realize is all they have is 100 percent. All they did by going extra hard to give 125 percent effort was show themselves what 100 percent actually looks like! You can't give 20 percent today and 180 percent tomorrow to make up for the lost effort. Life doesn't work that way. You can't make up tomorrow what you failed to give today.

Reaching your dreams will take everything you've got. You can't expect 100 percent reward with 70 percent effort. You can't expect to withdraw from life more than you deposit.

This story about one of my teammates illustrates the point perfectly. One day during a brutal workout, our strength coach asked us to finish the workout with four sets of 10 straight bar curls. I'll never forget cranking out my curls and looking across the room at my teammate. He did about three curls and as soon as the strength coach walked past him, he set down the bar and didn't finish his set. He looked at me and we both laughed. He laughed because he thought it was funny that he was skipping reps. I laughed because I thought it was a dumb decision—that work ethic wouldn't take him pro. He was like that at almost every workout. Fast forward to the end of our senior year. NFL scouts were set to come in six months to see all of our seniors work out. The teammate was training harder than I'd ever seen. He was working out two times a day and hired a professional trainer. He was posting workout clips on social media. He was G-R-I-N-D-I-N-G. Man, if he had worked like that since freshman year, he would have had a great chance of playing at the next level. But he tried to make up for four years of slacking in six months. It didn't work out. I admired his effort, and I'm not saying he shouldn't have trained the way he did those final months. I'm using his story to illustrate what can happen when you give less than your best. It may save some pain in the short term, but it will likely lead to regret later. Our goal should always be to give our best; our lives and the people we're called to impact deserve it.

And while we're here, let me note that rest should be included in your 100 percent effort. You don't have to burn the candle on both ends to be successful. You don't have to sleep four hours a day to make progress. Find a rhythm that works for your season of life and be content. Sometimes we as former athletes have a "no days off" or "all grind, no sleep" mentality that's very unhealthy. Giving 100 percent may be spending 24 hours with eight hours of sleep, eight hours of work, one hour of personal development, one or two hours of discretionary time and five hours of family time. That's OK. Giving 100 percent isn't about rushing the process either. You're not giving 100 percent effort because you want to reach your goal in one month instead of six. You're giving your 100 percent effort because that's what brings you fulfillment and produces maximum impact. Knowing you've worked hard, pushed your limits and tried your best is what enables you to sleep well at night because you've done your best with what you can control.

Which leads us to **mastering your time.**

In Today Matters, leadership expert John Maxwell writes, "We overexaggerate yesterday—past failures and successes. We overestimate tomorrow—things will get better; I will do it tomorrow. We underestimate today—don't recognize today's potential and value. So, what is the missing piece to your success? The secret to your success is determined by your daily agenda!"[17]

Pursuing your purpose requires you to master your time. Effective time management is based on goals and energy management, not tasks. Your purpose is your life's destination. Your goals are your pit stops. Your calendar is your roadmap.

In today's world there are literally thousands of digital and print time management tools. From online task managers to the old school pen and paper, the options can be overwhelming. I'm not going to get into what tool I believe is best. You can visit my blogs to see what works for me. The key is to find what works for you. The tool will be different for everybody, but the principles of time management are the same.

Setting goals

Goals help ensure you're creating the life you desire. They keep you focused. Many experts agree that people who set goals and take daily action toward reaching them are far more likely to succeed.

George T. Dornan's S.M.A.R.T. goals strategy is among the most popular and arguably the most effective.[18] Dornan says goals should be:

- Specific
- Measurable
- Attainable
- Relevant
- Time-based (Later adjustments suggest Time-Bound.)

Let's break these down a little.

Specific
The more specific you are in describing your goal, the greater chance you'll have to achieve it. Specificity brings clarity. It takes you from "I want to lose weight" to "I want to lose fat in my stomach and legs." Those

added details would help you tailor your workouts and nutrition plan, thus increasing your chances of accomplishing your specific goal.

To make your goals more specific, consider asking yourself the following questions:

- With whom?
- Where?
- How?
- Why do I want to accomplish this goal?
- What exactly do I want to accomplish?

Measurable

Making goals measurable means you'll need to find concrete ways to identify how you'll know if you've achieved them. It's what takes your goal from "I want to save money" to "I want to save $10,000." If you only say you want to save money, you'll never know when you've reached your goal. Making it measurable means you'll know when you've reached your goal so you can celebrate and set new goals.

Sometimes it helps to think about what you will see, hear and feel once you reach your goal. Let's say you have a goal to have a better marriage. To make it measurable, you could say that a better marriage for you would mean more laughter, face-to-face conversations and smiles. Then you could adjust your goal to "I want to see my spouse smile more. I want to create more moments of laughter and have face-to-face conversation every day." This description gives you a way to measure progress toward the goal—without being weird and tallying every time you see your spouse smile.

Attainable

This is where goal-setting becomes more of an art. The key is to find a balance between challenging yourself and fooling yourself. A challenging goal may be to obtain a bachelor's degree in three years. A foolish goal would be to obtain your bachelor's degree in six months.

I've seen people stand on opposite sides of the spectrum when it comes to setting attainable goals. Some people are so afraid to fail they set easy goals that never stretch them. Others are super zealous and set unrealistic goals that eventually discourage them when they get nowhere close to success. Learning how to set attainable goals may take practice. When I first started blogging, my goal was to post every day. I figured I could write a thorough blog post in one hour. I was wrong. Quality blogging took much longer. What I thought was attainable was unrealistic, so I had to adjust. Remember, you're learning about yourself as you pursue your purpose. Be flexible on the journey.

Relevant

This is making sure your goal is relevant to your life's purpose. Don't set a goal because of what everyone else is doing. If your goal is not connected to your life plan, accomplishing it would be pointless. Make sure the goal you set is worth your time and energy. Also, be sure all of your goals somewhat align to each other.

Don't set a goal to get a degree in video game production if you want to be a third-grade English teacher. One has nothing to do with the other. Don't set a goal to lose 10 pounds while also pursuing a goal of trying two new restaurants a week.

Time-bound

This is where you attach a target completion date. Rather than saying, "I want to write a book," you set a goal to write the first two chapters in the next two months. Attaching a completion date helps motivate you. The goal feels more realistic when you go from saying, "I'm going to do this," to saying, "I'm going to do this by this date."

Setting smart goals increases your probability of achieving them. It helps to write your goals on paper and find a creative way to keep them in front of you.

I review my goals daily to stay focused and make sure I don't mistake busyness for effectiveness. Sometimes we can be like hamsters on a wheel. Very busy. Exerting a lot of energy. And going nowhere.

Many people have modified Dornan's S.M.A.R.T. acronym, and one of my favorite adaptations is from Michael Hyatt and Company, who added two more elements—exciting and risky.[19]

Exciting

You should look forward to achieving your goal. You should actually want to achieve it versus dreading it. This gives you the necessary motivation and mindset to reach your goal, no matter the obstacles you face.

Risky

Your goal should stretch you. It should seem just a little impossible—but not so much that you don't believe you can achieve it. There will be days when you may think you've reached too far, but hang in there. You WILL make progress.

Our coaches used to say, "Work smarter, not harder." Use that same principle here to set S.M.A.R.T.E.R. goals that will take you to the next level of success.

Master your calendar

Schedule time to pursue your identified purpose. Use your SMARTER goals to determine what activities you schedule in your calendar. If your goal is to read a book a week, then schedule time to read a book. If your purpose is to empower children, schedule time to empower children. The adage is true. What gets scheduled gets done. Do not, I repeat, do not say, "I'll just grind as hard as I can every day. I don't need goals or a calendar." It sounds tough, my friend, but winging it is far from a foolproof plan. Grinding hard without a calendar is like trying to chop down a tree with a butter knife. You'll exert a lot of effort but won't make much progress. Many former athletes approach life after sports with the grind-hard mentality that was formed during many years of being an athlete. Most athletes just show up to workouts, practices, games, class and grind hard. What they don't realize is that the only reason they could do that is because somebody—a coach, an administrator, a teacher—put dates and times on a calendar.

I'll never forget the first time I watched from the press box my senior year as my team played. I was volunteering with the athletic communications team and observed all the administration that goes into making a college game run smoothly. I listened as our team planned the promotion, pregame media interviews, in-game entertainment and post-game recaps. I watched people unpack RVs for tailgating, walk from miles away to get free parking, shepherd their entire youth organization, and stand in line for hours at will call. I wondered why I'd never noticed any of this. As an athlete, I was always so focused on the game that I never noticed how much beauty was happening around me. I remembered the band playing, the ESPN cameras and the thousands of fans. But I never noticed all the business, administration and activities happening. I just showed up, worked hard, and the rest took care of itself. There was a system and structure surrounding the success of sports. Media knew where they needed to go and when they needed to be there. Police mapped the route teams would travel from hotel to field. Coaches scheduled when they would talk with each other and when they would meet with their position groups. Our pregame warmups? Scheduled. The duration of halftime? Planned. Post-game meal? Pre-ordered. Next practice? On the calendar. The athletes were just showing up while everyone else was following a plan.

Which goes to show you need a system to pursue your purpose. You need a game plan to succeed. Start by scheduling time to work intentionally toward your dreams.

Too many people quit chasing their dreams because they don't make progress as fast as they want. Setting goals and scheduling time on your calendar to pursue them are turbo boosters that will propel you to your destination faster.

Once you've set your goal-focused calendar, make sure every day to:

Reflect: Journal what you learned about yourself, how you can improve, where you wasted time, how you can be more efficient, and what you're doing that's working.

Adjust: Determine what you are going to do to get better.

Resume: Keep moving forward.

Your calendar could be the difference between building a life you love or living a life you hate. Coaches say you play how you practice. If you practiced taking short cuts as an athlete, then you'll probably struggle with finishing and consistency in your post-sports career as well. You can create better habits by scheduling intentional time to pursue your purpose.

Pursuing your purpose means you are writing your book, writing your business plan, studying for your test, practicing your speech, making sales calls, etc. You are doing the **most important activities to** get closer to your goal. Notice I said the most important, not the second-most important. One of Steven Covey's principles in *7 Habits of Highly Effective Leaders* is "first things first."[20] In this internationally best-selling book, Covey mentions that the opposite of putting first things first isn't putting first things last—it's putting first things second. Since you're going to be highly successful, you'll need to develop the habit of doing the most important things first.

As an athlete, your schedule was partially done for you. The schedule created for you helped you get better every day. The reason you had workouts at 5 a.m., a team meeting at 3 p.m., position meetings at 4 p.m., practice at 5 p.m. and film at 9 p.m. was that someone knew a calendar was of utmost importance if you and the team were going to be successful. A calendar is how you and your team got bigger, faster, stronger and more skilled. Thoughtful scheduling prepared you to pursue the goal of winning a championship.

The same principle of managing your calendar to navigate success applies to your life after sports. The major difference between your calendar in sports and your calendar after sports is who's in charge. In sports, a coach or administrator sets your agenda. After sports, **you** are the one scheduling what you will do and when. And when you really think about it, isn't it great to know you control your own progress? Isn't it awesome that you get to decide when you practice and how long? You get to choose how fast you move. You get to determine your practice drills. You have the power over your success in your own mind and hands.

You're in charge—make it count

I don't know about you, but I would have managed my schedule a little differently from my coaches. Why? Because I know myself better than anyone else. I know when it's best for my body to train and my mind to focus. If it were up to me, I would have completely flipped my schedule. I would have had film and classes in the morning and workouts and practices in the afternoon/evening. Why? Because my mind is most alert in the morning, and my body is more alert later in the day. Now you can't storm into your coaches' offices and demand to work out and watch film when it's best for you because that may not be what's best for the team. Life after sports is different from your life in sports, in part because you're no longer on a team—unless you've found a new team or joined our Second Chance Athletes movement.

As you pursue your purpose by being intentional with time, here's a fast-track tip: Schedule purpose time during your peak performance hours. If you're most alert in the morning, wake up early, and use that time to work toward your goal. When you do this, your results will multiply due to increased efficiency. I wish I had known this when I was getting started. I was working crazy hard to learn how to work in the corporate world and become an entrepreneur, but my progress was slow. I was being intentional. I scheduled my time, but I felt like there was more I could be doing. It was only after reading time management books and spending hours researching that I learned highly successful leaders achieve top performance by scheduling their most important tasks during peak times. They don't check emails, answer phone calls or peruse social media during those times. They strategically use their strengths then because they're at their sharpest, most alert and most effective.

As an athlete, I played better when our games were at night. When we had midday games at 2 or 3 p.m., I was more sluggish and tired. I'd been up all morning, and by the time the game rolled around, I was ready for a nap. My teammates would tell you I'd hurry up and get dressed for afternoon games and practices, then try to catch a quick nap in my pads before the action started. Just imagine all those other players listening to pregame music, jumping up and down, getting hyped and banging their heads on the locker ... and there I was, catching a quick nap! I never knew why I was so tired until I learned about peak performance times, which for me are from 5-11 a.m. and 8-10 p.m.

When I played sports, I couldn't change game or practice times, but now that my sports career is done, I get to choose when I practice, when I perform and when I take naps. You have the same control over your schedule and your success. You're the best person to lead the pursuit of your purpose. You've got this.

Invest in yourself

The most important investment you can make is in yourself. Why? Because you take you wherever you go. Every job, every relationship, every environment—you're the common denominator. You can trade cities, but you still take you with you. You can change relationships, but you still take you with you. You can make more money, but you're still the one managing it.

If you want a better life, start by becoming a better you. Here's a quick list of ways you can invest in yourself:

- Read print books, eBooks and audio books.
- Listen to podcasts.
- Watch personal development YouTube videos or webinars.
- Go to conferences.
- Pursue a formal education (GED, bachelor's, master's, doctorate).
- Practice your craft.
- Take online courses.
- Participate in seminars and workshops.
- Expose yourself to new environments.
- Get a mentor.
- Network with people who are doing what you wish you could do (or something similar).
- Join a professional development group.
- Eat healthy foods.
- Exercise regularly.
- Get 7 to 8 hours of sleep each night.

About your health

Investing in yourself means investing in your health. This includes physical fitness and nutrition. Many former athletes struggle with their health because they are so used to burning a lot of calories each day. After sports, that number dramatically decreases while their calorie intake often stays the same. This leads to weight gain and potentially a plethora of health issues. Many athletes tell me the changes in their bodies also decreases their self-esteem and causes depression because they don't look or function like they used to.

Nutrition and fitness are complex topics. Research changes all the time. Every workout or diet claims it's the best. I can't explain the science behind it all, although I will share my general observations regarding health and nutrition as they pertain to former athletes, including my own life as well as the lives of former athletes we've coached.

1. Prioritize nutrition.

Many health professionals agree the key to healthy weight loss is 80 percent nutrition and 20 percent fitness. This is a paradigm shift for a lot of athletes who were never taught about the importance of nutrition. My freshman year, I weighed somewhere between 209 and 217 pounds. I can't remember my exact weight (#concussions). Since I was 6'5" and had a large body frame, my coaches knew I easily could put on 50 to 60 pounds and be a beast of an athlete. They challenged me to gain one pound a week by eating whatever, whenever. If I weighed in at the end of the week and didn't meet my goal, they would make me run. Backward, right? Seems like they would make me lift, not run. Anyway, their scare tactic worked. I gained the weight, working my way up to 235, then 255, then 265 and finally 275. The problem is I developed very bad eating habits. Sometimes to gain weight, I would eat $12 to $15 of McDonald's because it was the closest restaurant to my dorm. That was two double cheeseburgers, chocolate chip cookies, a vanilla shake, large fries, large Pepsi and two apple pies. When I ate on campus, I would eat three servings and take eight to 10 cookies to go. Anybody who went to CMU knows their chocolate chip cookies SLAPPED! Slapped is an African American colloquialism used to describe a food or beverage that is very delicious.

Since I was working out and meeting my goal weight, I didn't think my eating habits were an issue. Then post-career came, and I gained a quick 15. I tried to work out but had no motivation, which I'll talk about shortly. I soon got married, had kids, and the next thing you know, I'd gone more than a year without working out. I lost muscle and replaced it with fat and a pudgy little "dad belly." I ended up weighing almost 290 pounds.

I never in my life thought I would get to the point where I was embarrassed to take off my shirt in public, but I did. I certainly didn't think that before age 30 I would be so out of shape and overweight that I couldn't dunk a basketball or run a half a mile without being out of breath. I was in bad shape, and I couldn't break free. I had no energy to work out. I hated healthy eating, I sucked at meal prepping, and exercising was discouraging.

Eventually, I found a health system that changed my life. I talk about it on my blog at secondchanceathletes. com. I lost 25 pounds in 40 days, cut three inches in my stomach and a ton of fat in other areas of my body. It was a game changer and the lifestyle boost I needed. The best part is that I still enjoyed in moderation most of the food I like (Chinese, ice cream, french fries, baked beans, mac and cheese, pulled pork, steak, etc.). And I did it through nutrition, not working out twice a day. I worked out 12 times during that 40-day period and experienced a much clearer mind and sustained energy levels.

The system I used made nutrition simple. It worked for me. The key is finding what works for you. Your results will multiply when you focus 80 percent of your healthy lifestyle habits on nutrition and 20 percent on physical fitness. Working out five days a week is important, but I know too many athletes who look healthy on the outside but have terrible eating habits. The consequences can be diabetes, liver failure, heart attacks, cancers and more. Invest in your health for the long term by making nutrition a priority today.

2. Take care of your injuries.
I have never met a former college, semi-pro or pro athlete who didn't have an injury at some point. My best advice is to take care of injuries just like you would if you were still playing sports. Do your rehabilitation exercises. Stretch every day. Continue to see a physical therapist. Do whatever is necessary to treat and heal your injuries.

I see too many athletes fall into the trap of ignoring their injuries because they're no longer preparing for competition. The next game is what motivated them to nurse their bodies back to health. When their career ended, they thought, "What's the point?" The point is that your body is important. And although the pain may be tolerable now, it will worsen if left untreated. Depending on your health insurance, you may have to pay a significant amount to properly treat your injuries. However, the cost of **not** taking care of your body will be far more costly. Chiropractic care is substantially less expensive than back surgery. Trust me! Make the investment in your long-term health. Do whatever you legally can to heal your injuries and ensure you can live a long, healthy, active life!

3. Try group exercises or competitions.
Some former athletes end up working out more after sports than they did when they played. They turn into

workout-aholics. Some become body builders. I wasn't one of those.

The first time I went to a gym after my football career, I got all dressed up to do an intensive workout. I had headphones on and was feeling great. Yet, when I finished my first set of exercises, I was bored.

I remember thinking:

- Why is the music so low in here?
- Why are there TVs playing sitcoms in the weight room?
- Why is that girl reading a book while walking on the treadmill?
- Would it be weird to ask one of the guys in the gym to come slap me on the chest and across the face to get my hype before I bench press? (It's a football thing.)

I couldn't take the "normal people" workout environment. I needed a bunch of people screaming at me to push the weight. I needed some high fives after my reps. I needed somebody to compete against or at least be around a bunch of people who were actually trying to go hard!

If this sounds like you, my advice is to join a group exercise program or workout competition. CrossFit is popular among former athletes, and although I've never tried it, I hear it's mad fun and energizing. Originally, workout videos worked best for me. They helped me feel like I was working out with a group of motivated people. That may be a good starting place for you. Do a Google search for group exercise or workout classes, and you'll find plenty of options. Sign up for a race. My first was a 5K. I was highly out of shape, but competing with someone old enough to be my grandpa was better than not competing at all. As a former athlete, use your competitive nature to your benefit! The debate among many former athletes is whether competition is a good or bad thing. Some say you shouldn't have to compete all the time. Others say being competitive is just what athletes do. Here's my opinion. Competitiveness is amoral. It's all about motive. If your motivation is to compete just to make someone feel terrible so you can feel better about yourself, that's unhealthy. If you compete just to have fun and win some bragging rights, that's healthy.

Quick funny story about unhealthy competitiveness

One day I was on a mile run trying to get back into shape. Some high school kid playing basketball on a raggedy hoop in the street started taunting me. He kept talking about how he could beat me one-on-one and that I was too afraid to play him. I laughed, ignored him and kept running. After I finished my workout, I started walking home to cool down. The boy was still talking junk, so this time I accepted his challenge. I figured it would make him happy and I could see if I still had it. We went back and forth for a few shots until I had the ball for the game-winning possession. At this point the kid was talking so much junk that I let my unhealthy competitiveness kick in and wanted nothing more than to embarrass him. His brother was watching, and I asked him to record the game-winning point. I noticed the rim was low … maybe 8.5 or 9 feet tall. I knew I could still dunk on that rim easily. I pump-faked. He jumped. I dribbled toward the basket. He ran to catch up. I jumped. He jumped. And he got dunked on. It felt great! I proceeded to talk smack in the camera and make sure his brother recorded his embarrassing nonsense excuses for getting dunked on. I posted that video on all my social media channels and had a blast responding to everyone's comments.

Fast forward a couple of months. The kid ends up going to church with me. I promise you I'm not lying when I say that 80 percent of the people I introduced him to said, "Oh yeah, that's the kid from your social media video that you dunked on." Some even laughed when they said it. The more people who addressed him as the kid I dunked on, the more ashamed he felt, which is not what you want your guest at church to feel. It was really getting to him, and there was nothing I could do to fix it. That's when I realized how unhealthy competitiveness can get. The good news is that kid got over it, and he and I are still close.

But I've seen unhealthy competitiveness destroy marriages, cause fights and end friendships. Check your motivation when you compete. Make sure your heart is in the right place. It would be tragic to pursue your purpose alone because you're too competitive to build intimate relationships. Use your competitive nature not to put others down and inflate your ego, but to drive you to get in shape and become the best version of yourself.

Find your tribe

You are the average of the five people you spend the most time with. It's not certain who came up with that statement. Some say motivational speaker Jim Rohn, so let's give him credit.

You may have heard it a billion times. I did. And it annoyed me. I dismissed it as a catchy saying but not truth. However, I came to a place in my life where I was stuck and couldn't figure out how to get to the next level. My progress seemed much slower than it should have been, and Jim Rohn's quote was the first thing that came to mind. I got out a piece of paper and wrote down my five closest friends. I estimated their salaries. I figured my salary was ... yep—you guessed it—the average of theirs. My social media followers ... the average of theirs. The health of my marriage was the same as the health of their marriages. My relationship with my children was the same quality as their relationship with their children. They say your network determines your net worth, which I found to be shockingly true. It was a humbling moment.

I realized how the people I was surrounding myself with was keeping me stagnant in life. Although they were good people whom I loved dearly, I had to find a way to be around people who were willing to evolve with me or who already had what I wanted in life and my relationships. I had to put myself in environments where I was afraid to speak because I wasn't the smartest or most skilled person in the room. They say if you're always the smartest person in the room, you're in the wrong rooms.

So, I started going in the right rooms. This was challenging, especially being a minority, because many minorities are conditioned to associate only with people who look and/or think like them. If a minority starts to hang around people who think and look different from their particular minority group, that person is considered to be a traitor. I was told I was acting "boojie,"[21] which is an African American slang word that means "too good for someone or a group of people." I was told I forgot where I came from—that I essentially was turning my back on my people by changing my relationships. The truth, though, was that I didn't forget where I came from. I just didn't want to stay there. I wasn't acting boojie or too good to hang around the people I grew up with. Our separation was taking place because I was choosing to evolve, and they were not. I had to shake free from the mindset I was being a traitor in order to move forward.

I started with my coworkers. Since they already knew me, I figured it would be easier than having lunch with a random CEO. I asked about their life, their upbringing, their thought patterns, their worldview and their passions. I became friends with a particular coworker and found out she had entrepreneurial dreams as well. She already had a website and online portfolio. I did not. I asked her about it, and she showed me how she did it. It was much simpler than I thought. I had put off creating my own website for almost two years because I thought I needed money and experience. Thanks to my coworker's advice, I was up and running within a week or so—all because I changed who I spent my time with.

And since I wanted to gain experience in public speaking, I volunteered for an organization led by a well-known motivational speaker. At that time, I had never earned any income from speaking because I didn't know what to charge and didn't think I was good enough for that. I had no clue how to put together a contract, negotiate a price and secure a gig. I asked if I could shadow him during his next speaking engagement. He said yes. When he had some down time, I asked him a ton of questions about speaking. He gave me great advice. Within a few months I got my first paid speaking gig for $500, then $1,000, $2,000, $3,000 and so forth. (I know some of you want to know how much I charge now. Guess you'll have to hire me to figure it out. :) #shamelessplug

The money and business and websites weren't the best parts. Who I was became more important than how much money I made. I formed relationships with people who had a better marriage than mine. When I saw how that husband treated his wife, it challenged me to treat my wife better. I treated her better, and she treated me better. Our marriage became stronger. I built relationships with people who had great relationships with their kids. When I saw how they had family traditions, time together without internet or mobile devices, game nights, reserved family time, etc., I found my own way to forge better relationships with my wife and children. It worked. Changing the people I spent my time with made me a better father, husband, entrepreneur and friend.

If you don't know where to look to find your tribe, we invite you to start with us. Maybe you don't trust the people around you, or maybe you've been abandoned by parents, friends, coaches and family. Second Chance Athletes is jam-packed with positive high achievers. We'd be happy to help you get connected and progress toward your goals. Shoot us an email, and we'll connect you with people who will push you forward instead of keeping you stagnant or pulling you backward.

Turn your athletic experience into after-sports success

Pursuing dreams after sports can seem overwhelming. You might feel like you're beginning at the bottom with a long way to climb. And while you do have a lot of work ahead, your starting point is not as far down as you think. Your experience as an athlete has prepared and positioned you for success.

In fact, many employers actively seek to hire former athletes because of the skills they acquired on teams and as competitors. Opinions and research vary on what Secret Sauce Skills former athletes have that employers want. Rather than find common denominators however,

I chose to list the top five that helped me and our Second Chance Athletes community excel in life after sports.

Top five Secret Sauce Skills of former athletes

1. Teachable

Or the word we athletes use is "coachable." It's the ability to receive feedback and instructions and make the necessary adjustments to improve our game. **As athletes, we don't just receive feedback, we crave it.**

This is different from the average professional who views constructive criticism as a negative. Athletes are wired for feedback. We critique and evaluate EVERYTHING. We're used to coaches examining the details of our work and screaming at us to correct the tiniest details. We are used to watching film and inspecting our movements and mindset so that we can get just 1 percent better at our craft.

This is what makes us great assets to employers and effective leaders in business. We're moldable. We don't get defensive when someone suggests ways we can improve. We have thick skin, and we'll take ruthless critique of our work because we know it makes us better.

2. Teamwork

If I had a dollar for every time I heard a coach say, "There's no I in team" or "Teamwork makes the dream work," I'd be a rich man. Teamwork is drilled into our psyche playing sports, and it's an asset we'll take with us wherever we go.

We know individual success produces team success. We know we're only as strong as our weakest link. We're not satisfied with win-lose scenarios. If we score 100 points in a basketball game, but lose, we're upset. If we score seven points and win, we're on top of the world.

Beyond working well with others, teamwork helps us overcome one of the greatest workplace challenges—silos. Organizational silos are a result of employees not understanding, valuing and prioritizing teamwork.

When you understand and foster teamwork, trust is high, conflict resolution is easier, and accountability is a given, in large part because teamwork means we're all in this together. If one of us is behind on reaching our goals, we all chip in and push the weary to get stronger. Teamwork is an innate default for the athlete, and it sets us apart from other professionals who have a hard time seeing the bigger picture.

3. Courageous leadership

Athletes are all about being No. 1. We're happy with winning records, but not satisfied. Our ultimate goal is to win championships. So, when we lead, we lead big. We lead to win. We lead courageously.

Plus, we're used to being leaders. When I speak to athletes, I always tell them that whether or not they want to be, they are leaders. Being an athlete automatically makes you one. No matter the level at which you play, the world we live in views athletes as role models. People wear our jerseys. Ask for our autographs.

Follow our social media accounts. More importantly, they watch us and listen to what we say. It's influence. And because we're used to being viewed as leaders, leadership becomes natural to us.

We're also good at managing multiple responsibilities. We're used to having practices, workouts, classes, homework assignments, media days, etc., and thriving in the chaos.

This is what makes us good leaders—courageous leaders willing to rally others and guide them toward big, scary, seemingly impossible goals.

4. Work ethic

Athletes are high-energy, intense, fast-paced individuals. How could we not be when we were challenged to wake up at 5 a.m., get ready, scarf down breakfast, rush to workouts, change our gear, push our bodies to the limit, stretch, shower, change, rush to class, listen, take notes, next class, next class, eat lunch, rush to practice, get changed, run drills to the point of exhaustion, shower, get dressed, eat dinner, watch film, study for tests, do homework, shower again, put on our jammies and do it again the next day … and the next day … and the next day. It's the fast-paced life of the athlete, and it gets more demanding at every level.

I'll never forget my first office job after sports and thinking:

- Why is it so dead in here?
- Why is everyone taking so long to get settled and start their day?
- Did they really just have a 40-minute conversation in the middle of the day?
- Did she just take a two-hour lunch and call it a meeting?
- Why does it take so long for decisions to be made?
- Why is a 15-minute meeting taking an hour?
- Are people even working?

The pace of the workplace was slow, and I hated it. Honestly, it's hard to find a non-sports organization that moves at the pace athletes and other driven people groups are accustomed to. That's one reason many athletes become coaches, work in the sports and entertainment industry or become entrepreneurs.

Our work ethic demands to be challenged in whichever career path we pursue. It gives us an edge among some professionals who haven't been forced to meet rigorous demands

5. Results-oriented resilience

Athletes and other high achievers have been coached and pushed to win, no matter the obstacles.

High achievers make a way where others may make excuses. They are great at performing under pressure, while others may cave under the weight of responsibility. Underdeveloped workers lose focus, become less effective and become timid when things get tough. It's the opposite for high achievers. Pressure makes them tougher, more focused and more competitive. They see obstacles as stepping stones rather than impossible barriers to climb. They keep our eyes on the prize and do whatever it takes to win.

Use these powerful traits to support your life after sports. They will help you walk in your purpose and achieve your goals.

My only warning is to be wise in how you deal with others.

Recognize that different people have different motivations. If you're married to someone who isn't an athlete or high achiever, don't attempt to force them to become one. Allow them to run at their own pace, and respect their unique strengths, talents and ambitions. Truthfully, they have strengths that you don't, and they most likely balance you out. Their goals may be different from yours, and if your idea of greatness isn't on their list, that's OK.

Every person matters. Use the skills that athletics ingrained in you to achieve success beyond the game. Just don't get prideful and make others feel inferior because they're not wired like you. We're all different. That's a good thing. Every piece of the puzzle deserves to be honored and celebrated.

Final thoughts on pursuit

Pursuing your purpose is a journey, not a destination. You need to become a lifelong learner in order to maximize your potential. Every person with a vision tries to rush the process. We want to upgrade our life as fast as we upgrade our cell phones. It doesn't work that way. Be patient with yourself as you build the life of your dreams. You may not be who or where you want to be yet, but be thankful you are no longer where or who you used to be. Take it from a suicide survivor that every day, no matter how bad, is worth cherishing. Enjoy your journey. Don't compare your pace to anyone else. Run your race. Take pleasure in every step.

Let's practice:

1. **What are you willing to go through in order to achieve your destiny?**

2. **What might you have to sacrifice to pursue your purpose?** Television? Fast food? Work benefits? Insurance? Your ego?

3. **What do you have that you may be overlooking?** A pencil? A computer? A relationship?

4. **How can you use what you have, where you are, to move forward?** Pencil + paper =

a book. Computer + google = grant money. Relationship + a question = opportunity.

5. **Write down your peak performance time.** If you don't know, make a guess. You can always change it.

6. **Set 30-day, 90-day, 1-year, 5-year and 10-year goals.**

7. **Schedule your most important tasks based on your goals.** Reserve space for them in your calendar during your peak performance times.

8. **Reflect, adjust, resume.**

9. **Choose three ways to start investing in yourself.**

10. **Brainstorm people you can connect with who will become your new team.**

11. **Strategize how you can leverage your athletic traits to produce success in your life beyond sports.**

CHAPTER 7
PERSIST TO BECOME ELITE AGAIN

The big questions:

1. Why don't I feel like building my dreams anymore?

2. Why does it seem like I never have enough money or resources?

3. How do I stay motivated?

The goal:

To have a strategy to keep you going when life gets tough and you're tempted to quit on your journey to become elite again. Persistence is the key to going through the fifth and final step of The Athlete Transition Roadmap.

Leadership expert John Maxwell says, "Motivation gets you going, but discipline keeps you growing." That's a simple but profound truth, and it's easier said than lived.

You've heard the statistics of how the majority of people who make New Year's resolutions never accomplish them. It's not because they weren't motivated. On the contrary, they were ecstatic. They said, "New year, new me," or "This is the year I'll finally do (blank)." They started chasing their dreams and made it a month or so before their motivation dwindled, and their consistency diminished.

Some gym membership facilities book over their capacity because they know people who buy memberships in January are likely to stop coming in February. Every athletic team chants "champions on three" before their workout or practice. They warm up, shout and get all excited because this is going to be their championship year. Yet, before the workout is finished, they're complaining about its intensity and skipping reps. They had the motivation to get started but not the persistence to continue.

Use motivation as ignition and not as fuel

Success requires you to learn how to control your feelings and not allow your feelings to control you. You've got to do what's necessary even if you don't feel like it. In the sports culture, the fuel of the athlete's effort primarily consists of motivation. This is why we have pregame huddles and music, chants, chest bumps, high fives, a band playing and fans cheering. Athletes feed off the energy of their environment. This is where the term "home court advantage" comes from. Teams generally play better at home because they have more people cheering them on, motivating them to jump higher, run faster or swing harder. All the excitement is cool until the hype creates a subtle internal belief that performance is dictated by motivation. Many athletes live with the narrative of "I perform better when people cheer for me." Or, "I can't work hard unless I'm amped up and motivated." That internal narrative can become a belief that sabotages your success and prevents you from reaching your full potential. I'm not saying encouragement is bad or motivation isn't important. The high fives, loud music, speeches and cheers are great. Just don't use motivation as your fuel—use it as your ignition.

Let's face it. Sports isn't only a passion or a competition. It's entertainment. Throughout your competition there's music, fans, commercial breaks, performances, fan games, timeout chants and highlight films. The atmosphere in a sports arena is nearly impossible to compete against, and that's why there will never be anything quite like sports.

You'll be lucky to get a high five at the office, let alone a T-shirt cannon when you complete a project. Work and life after sports can be almost depressing in comparison. There's no dance team on your lunch break, no band playing when you send an email and no news reporters waiting when you clock out. If you're like me, you could find yourself feeling highly unmotivated to get up and go to work because of the lack of hype in the real world. I found myself being less productive, and I went through a season where I was trying to transform my work culture into a sports arena. I would play music, call huddles at work and try a bunch of tactics to get people pumped up. It definitely made work better for those who participated in my spontaneous chants and push-up challenges, but it was a failed attempt at creating the same motivating environment on my job that I had in sports. I had to learn to use motivation as my ignition and stop depending on it to be my fuel.

Fix your focus

We've settled the fact that it's difficult for daily life to produce the same level of motivation as the sports arena. So, how do you go the distance without depending on motivation to keep you running? How do you do what you need to do, even when you don't feel like doing it? How do you persist in the pursuit of your purpose?

Fix your focus on purpose, not process. Fix your focus on destination, not your situation. Focus on promises, not problems; on rewards, not risk. Focus is a magnifier. If you focus on problems, they'll grow larger in your mind, even though in reality they remain the same. If you focus on how hard a project or goal is, it will seem to get harder and more complicated. You've heard the saying, "If it's meant to be, it's meant to be." Well, I don't think that statement applies to everything. People often use that statement to justify inaction. It takes the blame off them and puts it on God or the universe. It makes people feel better, but it doesn't help them become better. I say if it's meant to be, act like it. Start by fixing your focus.

Think about a time when you skipped a rep, didn't touch the line, or didn't train as hard as you intended. What were you focusing on when you pulled back or quit?

More than likely you were focused on the pain and not the reward. You were focused on your arms hurting, your legs being sore, or your teammate cheating on all her reps. So you pulled back or stopped short. You allowed pain, not reward, to determine your grit. Imagine how different your results would have been if you'd focused instead on winning the championship, breaking the record, or dominating your opponent.

Focusing on rewards more than pain or process helps you persist when things get tough.

The first time a client asked me to facilitate a full-day marketing workshop, I told him how honored I was to have the opportunity. I got excited about adding value to all the participants. I was so happy and joyful until … it hit me … I had never trained anyone how to market effectively. I had no clue how to facilitate a full-day workshop. I had a hard time putting together a 30-minute keynote. How in the world was I going to talk for eight hours!? My excitement spiraled into anxiety. I researched and researched. Every expert had a different opinion about how to market effectively. Every workshop was different. There was no one right way to follow. I downloaded PowerPoints, watched Ted Talks and skimmed books, but the more I read, the more confused I got.

I started to focus on all the complications. I asked myself questions like:

- What if we get done four hours early?
- What if no one participates in the activities?
- What if I forget my train of thought and can't pick it back up?

Then those thoughts morphed into self-defeating statements like:

- I should cancel the workshop and **quit** my business.
- I don't have enough experience or education to teach people how to market effectively.
- I have no clue what I'm doing. I don't have what it takes.

That negative focus was causing me to subconsciously self-sabotage my success. Luckily, I prayed, calmed down and made up my mind to stick with it.

I shifted my focus to my purpose with statements like:

- I am gifted to teach and train people how to market effectively.
- I'm a creative marketing professional with mad ideas that can benefit others.
- I have more than enough experience to add value to others and facilitate a full-day workshop.
- I have what it takes to be an international speaker and consultant.

Can you guess what happened? Instead of quitting, I went through with it and have trained hundreds of people since then on how to market effectively. Oh yeah. And I got paid a premium, too!

This is the power of fixing your focus from process to purpose.

Persistence requires accountability

No one person is an island. The term "self-made" is a fallacy. The phrase "I don't need anybody" is a doctrine of failure. Everybody needs someone. Every Batman needs a Robin. Even the Lone Ranger had a horse. We all need somebody in our lives to hold us accountable for what we set out to accomplish.

According to the American Society for Training and Development, people who have an accountability partner are 85 percent more likely to succeed than those who only have an idea.

Identifying an accountability partner will help you to keep chasing your dreams even when life gets hard.

An accountability partner will remind you of the goals you set out to achieve. He or she will help pick you up when you can't do so yourself. Your accountability partner can be, but doesn't have to be, your best friend or closest companion.

An accountability partner is someone who:

- Desires to see you succeed
- Has your best interests in mind
- Knows your strengths and weaknesses
- Will speak the truth even if you won't like it

The American Management Association surveyed executives, managers and employees from more than 500 U.S. companies on the topic of accountability. A full 70 percent of respondents said a lack of accountability damages the overall performance of their organization.[22] Without an accountability partner, you'll be more vulnerable to your weaknesses. Without an accountability partner, you can start out trying to have a great marriage but end up having a devastating affair. Without an accountability partner, you can set out to write a book, but it never gets published. Your accountability partner will help you stay committed to your vision and core values. He or she will help you keep chasing your dreams when everything in you wants to quit. When you start to gain weight even though you said this was the year you were going to lose 10 pounds, your accountability partner will say, "Hey, I see you're starting to gain a little weight and haven't been working out as much. I'm just checking to make sure you're all right because I know you truly want to lose weight."

When you set a goal to save $10,000 but decide to go on an unnecessary shopping trip, your accountability partner will say, "Shopping is great, but do you think that's smart considering you're trying to save $10,000 this year?"

An accountability partner keeps you from sabotaging your success or ruining your reputation by making decisions that are counterproductive to your dreams and core values. Don't get me wrong, having an accountability partner isn't a fool-proof plan. You have to do your part, which is to:

- Be transparent: An accountability partner can't hold you to what you hide. You have to be transparent about your goals and your struggles.
- Be humble: An accountability partner can prescribe the medicine you need but can't make you take it. You have to listen and receive wisdom—especially when you don't want to be corrected.

Manage your money, or your money will manage you

In order to persist toward your dreams, you have to manage your money. Without proper money management knowledge and skills, you'll be like a hamster on a wheel—making a lot of effort but going nowhere.

Money isn't everything, but it definitely helps to have it.

My financial situation was one of the reasons I struggled with depression after my sports career ended. I was broke and constantly tormented by thoughts of what I could have been making had I been able to play professionally. I went from free school, free rent, free meals and Pell Grant checks to paying for everything myself. I spent months feeling hopeless and helpless because I thought sports was my only way to generate massive income. I wasn't good enough at anything else.

I TRIED "stacking my bread" (aka saving money). But then I spent it faster than I saved it.

I TRIED getting a better paying job. But the more money I made, the more money I spent. The popular saying "more money, more problems" was my reality. As soon as I started making more money, the car needed to be repaired, my family/friends "needed" to "borrow" some money, and random bills started coming in the mail.

I WAS SICK of watching my hard-earned money get swallowed by high rent, expensive utility bills, and other people's emergencies.

I knew there had to be something I could do to better my financial situation.

I was right. There was. It was called budgeting.

I had never tried budgeting because it seemed complicated, and I managed everything in my head. But once I started budgeting my money, the results were stunning.

- I had more money.
- I had more peace.
- I had more confidence.

Did I mention I had more money?

- I discovered ways to cut expenses.
- I recovered money from unauthorized transactions on my account.
- I stopped over-giving to people for their "emergencies."
- I paid off debt.
- I increased savings.

Did I mention I had more money?
And here's the best part: I had more money without making more money. Because budgeting helped me keep more of what I made.

I'm living proof that budgeting works. Check out what the professionals say:

- Budgeting helps you save money.—Turbo Tax[23]
- The average family pays off $5,300 and saves $2,700 in the first 90 days of taking Dave Ramsey's Financial Peace University, which features a zero-based budgeting system.—Dave Ramsey[24]
- Budgeting adds to your savings and gives you the freedom to use some money just for fun.—Forbes[25]

According to numerous resources, including Geir Management, even professional athletes need a budget.[26]

- 60 percent of NBA players file bankruptcy within five years of retirement.
- 78 percent of NFL stars will file for bankruptcy within five years.
- MLB players file for bankruptcy four times more often than the average U.S. citizen.[27]

Why? How? In part, because they don't have a budget.
"Most athletes have no idea what's going on with their money."—Intuit Mint[28]
If professional athletes with an abundance of money need a budget, so do you. Do a Google search, and you'll find plenty of free budgeting information and tools. We have a few free resources on our website that are simple and easy to use.

Mastering your budget will enable you to:

- Have more money without making any more than you make right now.
- Know exactly how you're spending your money so you can make changes and start saving.
- Set you on track toward reaching your financial goals.
- Help you pay off debt, and more.

Don't fall victim to the poverty mindset that thinks, "I don't need a budget; I just need more money." People struggling with a poverty mindset wait for more money. People with an abundance mindset understand the stewardship principle—doing better with what you have will attract more of what you want.

You can either avoid the hard work of creating and sticking to a budget while waiting for a major promotion or hoping to hit the lottery, or you can get control of your money, start saving and become a better steward of your finances.

There's plenty more to learn about financial management and wealth creation, but budgeting should be the first step. It will make sure you don't run out of gas before you reach your destination. Too many people complain a lack of money is keeping them from pursuing their dreams. My theory is the real culprit is a lack of financial stewardship. Learning to steward your money not only positions you for increase but also prepares you for increase. How you manage $10,000 will likely be how you manage $1 million. More money won't fix bad money habits. That's why, according to National Endowment for Financial Education, 70 percent of people who win a lottery or get a big windfall end up broke in a few years.[29]

Your purpose is too important to allow poor financial stewardship to keep you stuck in life. Maximize what you have, and you'll always have enough to keep moving forward.

Celebrate your wins

It's easier to see your progress in sports than it is to see your progress in life. In athletics, you measure everything. You measure how high you jump, how fast run, how accurate you punch and how much you lift. You record how much you weigh, the size of your waist, the size of your chest, the size of your neck and arms. You chart wins, losses and a plethora of game statistics. The sports life is filled with measurements, which makes it easy to track progress. And progress helps you persist in your process because you receive feedback on how you're doing.

Some things in life are hard or nearly impossible to measure. You have to be intentional about tracking what you can, so you'll stay inspired. Make sure you don't get so caught up in the destination that you neglect to celebrate the wins along the way. Record every win and try to celebrate often. You celebrated every competition you won. Make sure you celebrate your wins in life after sports as well.

Life doesn't play fair. You're going to experience failures and trials. And if you don't have a way to remind yourself about the times you won, your subconscious will remind you of the times you lost. Your wins in life will help you keep pressing toward your goals. You may not to be where you want to be yet, but recording your wins will show how far you've come from where you started. Write your wins down. Don't track them in your head because you'll forget them. And when you record your wins, be a little descriptive. Don't just write "booked the contract." Describe how you felt before you booked it. What were your fears? How much work did you put in? What did booking the contract do for your business or family? Being descriptive will help you connect with that win at a later time. When you're descriptive, you'll be able to review your wins during a difficult period in life and instantly be encouraged by reliving those great moments all over again. You'll remember why that win was so significant. You'll remember that you booked the contract right after an all-night argument with your spouse. Then, if you get in another argument later down the line, instead of looking for a divorce lawyer, you'll remember the time you had a win right after a big argument. You won't quit the relationship; you'll know an argument is part of the journey.

Athletes are some of the most resilient people on the planet. We constantly push our bodies to new limits. We keep going when we want to quit. We press harder. We find a way to keep going. Persistence isn't something you do. It's part of who you are.

You've got this. You were made for this.

Take care of you

One of my struggles after sports was learning how to take care of my internal wellbeing and not just my external wellbeing. I was good at physical conditioning; I had a work ethic that resulted in success, and I was social enough to have some good relationships. The problem, though, is that it's possible to do well on the outside but still be miserable on the inside, mentally and emotionally. To live your best life, you have to be emotionally healthy.

Emotional health frees you from ignored or suppressed emotions. It's ensuring that your heart isn't contaminated with bitterness, anger, jealousy, unforgiveness, self-hatred or anything else toxic.

It's so easy to ignore this tip. Athletes rarely slow down long enough to process our emotions. We bottle everything up and keep plowing through life. Society often views people who are in touch with their emotions as being weak. That couldn't be further from the truth. **Being in touch with your emotions doesn't make you weak. It makes you aware.** Being controlled by your emotions, including anger, is what makes you weak. Many former athletes struggle with anger because they never learned to display any other emotion. They get mad when they lose. They get mad when a teammate makes a mistake. They get mad when their coach yells at them. They get mad when they miss a play. Even the occasional cry after a loss is more of an angry cry then a sad cry. This is why many athletes don't want to be bothered after a loss. They want to be left alone. Keep messing with them, and you'll find out they're angry.

Administrators made me angry

I struggled with anger a lot after sports. I was angry at the world because of my injury. I was angry at myself for not finding a way to continue to play. I was furious at my coaches and administrators for not taking more interest in me as a person.

Our team had an annual banquet for the players and family where we celebrated the season, distributed awards and honored seniors by watching their career highlight video, allowing them to speak and giving them their helmet on a plaque. It was a special moment for everyone, especially the seniors.

I'll never forget the day I found out I wasn't invited to my senior banquet. My roommate came out of his room wearing black dress pants and a white dress shirt. Knowing he never dressed like that, I asked where he was going.

"What do you mean," he said, while adjusting his black tie.

"What do you mean, what do I mean? Why are you all dressed?" I asked sarcastically.

"To the banquet, bro. Aren't you going?" he said with equal sarcasm.

"The banquet?"

It hit me. He was talking about our senior banquet. And, we both knew in that moment that my coaches had forgotten to invite me.

"You know you can still come, bro. They would want you there," he said empathetically.

I thought about going but didn't want to face the embarrassment of not having a helmet, a highlight reel, or a place at the seniors table because my coaches and administrators forgot me.

"It's whatever, man. Forget them," I said.

Then I moved on.

So I thought.

Six months later it really started to bother me. Not only did I miss sports like crazy, but not participating in the senior banquet left me without closure. I was angry. I didn't get to play my last game on senior night. My last game was playing through unbearable pain for a quarter and a half and being benched the second half. I couldn't travel with the team my senior year because my scholarship had ended because I was no longer competing. That meant instead of taking 12 credits in the fall and five to seven credits in the spring, I would have to take 17 to 19 credits in the fall while working an internship. And they never even noticed they forgot me. I would have felt better if they had apologized, given me a helmet and let me say a few words to my team—but they didn't. The anger worsened as I remembered how much my coaches and administrators were interested in me when I was competing. They regularly asked how my family was doing. They checked in to see how I was doing. They praised my progress in the weight room. They made sure I had food to eat and stayed on top of my schoolwork. They seemed to care so much. Yet, when I could no longer help them win games, they forgot me. It was as if I never existed.

No phone calls to see how the injury was healing. No texts to say they missed seeing me on the field. No invitation to the bowl game—in the Bahamas! No complimentary bowl gifts. No senior banquet invitation. No highlight reel. No helmet!

The more I thought about all of that the more furious I became. I was killing it at my internship, earning the opportunity to be involved with a lot of writing/ PR assignments for Gen. Colin Powell's visit to CMU, but emotionally I was wrecked.

It was a terrible place to be. I smiled every day at work and went to bed every night depressed. Finally, the internal anger and bitterness was too much to bear. It dominated my life, and I couldn't do anything without thinking about it.

I scheduled a meeting with our head coach and told him how hurt I was that they forgot me and how I could never get that moment back. He apologized and felt terrible. He made sure I got my helmet and allowed me to address the team at the next banquet since I had played with many of those guys, too. It wasn't the same as being with the class I came in with, but it was better than nothing. Just getting the bitterness out of my heart was enough to celebrate. Getting bitterness and unforgiveness out of your heart is important to live mentally healthy and free. There's a common saying that "unforgiveness is like drinking poison hoping the other person will die." This lets us know that bitterness hurts no one but us. We often remain angry and unforgiving because we feel like we're punishing the person who offended us. Or, we think the only way for us to heal is to get a heartfelt apology from the person who wronged us. The problem is that the heartfelt apology may never come, and every second we spend thinking about the bad things that happened to us is a second wasted that we could be spending on positive thoughts that push us forward.

The fact that I was real about how I felt by not being invited to my senior banquet was liberating. I could attend meetings at work without battling bitterness in my heart. I could hear my coaches' names mentioned without wanting to bad-talk them. I forgave my coaches and administrators and realized they had made a terrible, but honest mistake. They felt horrible, and there was no reason to try to make them feel worse. My being mad at them was only making me angrier. Forgiving them released them and cleared my heart of the clutter.

That was a defining moment because it helped me realize the importance of emotional health. It's impossible to be completely fulfilled if you're struggling emotionally. It's hard to keep moving forward when your past still has its claws in your heart. It's like sprint training with a parachute. You'll progress, but you'll never move as fast or as long as you could if you lose that weight.

What's your parachute? A loss you never got over? An award you never received? A coach who betrayed you? A father who left you?

We've all had pain that left us with wounds beyond words. Yet it's one thing to get hurt, and it's another to stay hurt. At some point, we must choose to stop being the victim and choose to be the victor. We have to stop replaying our past, reliving our pain and masking our brokenness with busyness. We have to release our parachute.

Yes, we'll likely need to have difficult conversations with people who hurt us. And, not all of them will go as well as mine did with my coach. Sometimes those conversations will cause more pain than relief. But in the long run it will be worth the hurt. For some of us, the opportunity to talk with someone who hurt us doesn't exist. Maybe the coach moved and changed his number. Maybe the father is someone you never knew. In that case, I suggest you talk to a trusted friend or a counselor. Get it off your chest, and more importantly, out of your life. You need all of you to face the battles of your future. You need your whole self to persist through whatever life puts in your way. The heartache of processing your pain is worth the reward. Take it one wound at a time. One day at a time. One conversation at a time. Sooner or later your heart will be without open wounds. You'll still have scars. But you'll be emotionally healthy and ready to take on the world.

Know what refuels you

Life can be really tough at times. There will be moments when you feel like quitting, even when you know why you do what you do. It will feel like you've given everything and have nothing else to offer. Here's what helps me refuel and bring my A-game each day. I suggest you follow my Grid Iron Journal Method (listed below).

Write down what refuels you. Make lists, record victories and memories. And keep the journal handy.

Hobbies

All work and no play, grind hard, no sleep might be the worst advice ever. You need activities that refresh your emotions, reset your mind and rest your body. A lot of former athletes still like to engage in sports. I love to bowl and play basketball. I'm not in a league or anything, I just enjoy the sports. I love making music and going to movies. These activities refresh me. The key is to find things outside of work that nourish you.

Music

Music is powerful. It has the ability to alter your mood in seconds. I've seen music make people do crazy things. I've seen friends get into fights for no reason other than a rap song made them all hyped up to the point where they made wrong decisions. I've seen a football team come from behind and win because of a song that played during a timeout. R&B music has a way of setting the mood for slow dancing. Have you ever noticed how important music is in a movie? It enhances what's happening. Music can turn a happy person sad and a sad person happy. Use it for your good. Use it to pick you up when you're down. To energize you when you feel depleted.

Have you ever heard the song, "If you're happy and you know it, clap your hands?" Try singing that entire song when you're upset, and I guarantee it will be nearly impossible to stay mad. I have several playlists on YouTube and many albums on iTunes that were created to help me get into certain moods. When I don't feel like writing, even though I know it can help millions of people, I go to my writing playlist. A few instrumentals in, and I'm focused and ready to go. I have playlists to get me in the frame of mind to do administrative tasks. I have workout playlists, a chores playlist, a play with kids playlist, a snap out of negativity playlist, etc. Find the songs that put you in the right mood for the right task.

Laughter
Laughter is medicine to the soul. Science proves that laughter causes us to take in large amounts of air and oxygenate the blood. It decreases stress hormones, strengthens our immune system and releases "feel-good" hormones called endorphins.

Find out what makes you laugh, and make sure you can access it at a moment's notice. I can't tell you how many times I didn't feel like waking up, or I was so depressed I couldn't sleep, and I watched something funny which instantly brought me out of my sorrow.

Some ideas to make you laugh would be:

- A journal of funny life moments as part of your own Grid Iron Journal.
- Standup comedy
- Friends who make you laugh
- Photo album of funny pictures
- Comic strips
- TV shows
- Pets
- Children

Quotes
Just like music has power, so do words. There's something about a profound statement that centers your mind on what matters most. I have literally thousands of quotes that I can access instantly in my Grid Iron

Journal. Reading and reciting them, many from memory, almost always helps me stay persistent. Here are 10 of my go-to quotes.

1. "The jump is so frightening between where I am and where I want to be. But because of all I may become, I will close my eyes and leap!" —Mary Anne Radmacher[30]

2. "A righteous person falls seven times but gets back up."—King Solomon [31]

3. "Do it afraid."—Every motivational speaker in the world

4. "Never let a bad day make you feel like you have a bad life."—Darryll Stinson[32]

5. "If you are more fortunate than others, build a longer table, not a taller fence."—multiple

6. "Sometimes when you are in a dark place, you think you have been buried, but actually, you have been planted."—Christine Caine[33]

7. "Whenever you find yourself doubting how far you can go, just remember how far you have come. Remember everything you have faced, all the battles you have won, and all the fears you have overcome."—N.R. Walker[34]

8. "Sometimes it takes an overwhelm- ing breakdown to have an undeniable breakthrough."—multiple[35]

9. "Our deepest fear is not that we are inade- quate. Our deepest fear is that we are pow- erful beyond measure. It is our light, not our darkness, that most frightens us. Your playing

small does not serve the world. There is nothing enlightened about shrinking so that other people won't feel insecure around you. We are all meant to shine as children do. It's not just in some of us; it is in everyone. And as we let our own lights shine, we unconsciously give other people permission to do the same. As we are liberated from our own fear, our presence automatically liberates others."—Marianne Williamson[36]

10. "If you can't fly, run. If you can't run, walk. If you can't walk, crawl. But by all means, keep moving."—Martin Luther King Jr.[37]

Rest

Rest is to the body what sharpening is to the sword. Bestselling author Stephen Covey says, "Sharpening the saw means preserving and enhancing the greatest asset you have—you."

Whoever started the "no days off" movement must have been insane. Research has chronicled the impact that a lack of quality rest has on people of all ages. Quality sleep has been proven to reduce brain fogginess, illnesses, stress and numerous other health issues.

Without regular quality rest, you will not have the strength you need to maximize every day. You'll waste days and eventually begin to dread life. I've seen too many leaders quit work and give up on important relationships because they never made rest a priority. Most research suggests we should sleep seven to nine hours a day to function at our best.

Schedule a weekly rest day

For me, quality rest also means that I have one day a week where I don't work. I get extra sleep, reflect on life and do something that relaxes my body and fills me up. I try to spend time outdoors and allow nature to refresh me.

I also schedule staycations, retreats and vacations on my calendar.

Staycations = at-home vacations. Sometimes I rent a local hotel if it's in my budget to do so. Staycations usually last one to three days, and I find this is the most affordable and convenient way to rest.

Retreats = Three- to five-day getaways. I like to travel outside of my city and find a place that has warm weather, great facilities and nice outdoor scenery options. Vacations = Seven days or longer. It usually takes two or three days to completely disconnect from work.

I prefer two-week vacations when possible.

To maximize my rest, I do my best to disconnect from technology as much as possible. It's so important to disconnect from the busyness of life in today's culture where there are so many distractions from smart devices and the internet. You have to be intentional about when you're going to rest. If you wait until the perfect time, you will never rest, and you'll risk burnout. If you wait until work slows down or the kids get older, you may not ever make it. Be intentional about rest. You deserve it. Your purpose requires it. And, the people you impact deserve the "full you," not the half-rested, running-on-fumes you.

My secret weapon

There have been rare moments when no matter what I do, I can't seem to get out of feeling like I'm running on empty and want to retire from life and escape to a private island forever. It's in these moments that I pull out my secret weapon—my Grid Iron Journal. It's filled with favorite memories and defining moments.

I date and title each entry. Sometimes I jot bullet points about why that memory was so important to me. Most times I write a descriptive paragraph detailing my emotions in that situation.

I never make it through more than two pages in this journal without gaining the energy to keep pushing. It's like CPR to my soul. Reading about these moments in my life helps me relive them, as if they are happening in the present. I highly recommend you create a Grid Iron Journal. And don't neglect to make note of the emotions you experienced because they'll bring those moments to life and help shift your mood and mindset to a positive and energizing place of gratitude.

Let's go to work:

1. **Write down your purpose statement from chapter three.** Get it professionally designed by a graphic designer, print it on large paper or poster board and post it at your workplace. Use it to help you stay focused on purpose and thrive through the process.

2. **Write down five to ten core values**. Core values are principles you stick to no matter the circumstances. Make a commitment to honor your core values, whether you're motivated to or not.

3. **Find an accountability partner to help you follow through on your commitments.**

4. **Find a journal to record all your wins.** Be descriptive. Review regularly.

5. **Become a great steward of money.** Create a budget and weekly cashflow plan.

6. **Pay attention to your emotional health.** What wounds have you received from your past? Write a plan to become more emotionally healthy.

7. **Make a list of things that refuel you.** Keep them close and easy to access when you need them.

CHAPTER 8

JOIN THE MOVEMENT

From little league to the pros, every athlete's career will end. Some athletes prepare for life after sports. Some don't. Some struggle mentally. Others struggle physically. Some barely struggle at all.

Whether it's a lot or a little, I want you to know you're not alone.

The end of my athletic career almost cost me my life. I would be dead if it weren't for the life-changing experience I talked about in the chapter "What Really Happened?"

It's OK if you're struggling with life after sports.

It's OK to struggle, but it's not OK to stay silent about that struggle.

There are millions of former athletes in the world who are struggling and settling.

They're settling for jobs instead of chasing dreams.

They're settling for popularity instead of striving for significance.

They're settling for who they were instead of discovering who they are.

This is why we've launched a movement.

A movement of athletes who know there's more to their identity and life than sports.

This is why we've created a community.

A community of athletes who won't allow people to settle for average.

This is why we've created an army.

An army of athletes who are radical enough to believe that pursuing their purpose will result in changing the world.

If you know or would like to discover that there's more to your identity than sports, join our movement.

If you refuse to die average, join our team.

If you're bold enough to believe pursuing your purpose will result in changing the world, join our army.

Upon joining, you'll:

- Network and build camaraderie with thousands of current and former college and pro athletes from across the globe.
- Receive the latest transition content to help you advance your career and live both physically and mentally healthy.
- Find new identity and purpose beyond sports so you can build your legacy and live a fulfilled life.

The services and resources we offer are constantly growing and adapting to best meet the needs of our athletes. At the time of publishing this book we offer a free private Facebook community, group coaching, one-on-one coaching, on-site & virtual workshops, and online courses. Visit secondchanceathletes.com for more.

We've been able to help our clients eliminate after sports depression, start and grow businesses, secure their dream jobs, overcome depression and anxiety, spend more time with their families and simply live a happier and satisfied life.

Wherever you go from here, please don't settle. Don't just read this book and go back to life as usual.

Dig deep to discover your purpose and build a life beyond your wildest dreams.

And always remember that it's never too late to be great.

It doesn't matter what you've been through or how many mistakes you've made.

Life has a way of awarding us "second chances." And second chances exist so we can finish strong. Finish strong, my friend.

I was a complete mess when I walked into her house. I had been crying the entire way there, so my eyes were swollen, making them hard to keep open. My body was relapsing, and I had not eaten anything for two days. The last time she saw me, I was a 275-pound stud. This time I was 219 pounds and frail from trying to starve myself to death.

She tried to feed me, but I was so depressed I didn't have an appetite.

I was filled with self-hatred because I felt I had wasted my entire life striving to become a professional athlete and failed.

I was broken and furious that the woman I had planned to marry, my girlfriend of four and a half years, had left me and got engaged to another man. I had no desire to live without sports. I didn't want a boring corporate life. I was tormented by the reality that the two things I loved most in my life—sports and my girl-friend—were stripped away from me with no hope of coming back. I was too injured to ever play competitively, and no matter how much I begged and threatened to kill myself, my girlfriend wouldn't come back to me.

I couldn't take it. The pain of living was too extreme, and I wanted nothing more than to find rest in death. I rushed out the door as soon as my mother fell asleep. I was getting back in my car to finish what I originally set out to do. My mother heard the screen door fling open. She jumped out of bed, ran outside and pushed me away from the car. I tried to move her out of the way, but she was determined not to let me die. She begged me to allow her to take me somewhere to get some help. Once again she was convincing. I got in her car not knowing where she was taking me. I was ashamed and embarrassed that I was acting so out of character. I covered my face and cried the entire commute. By the time we got to the hospital, I could barely see. My eyes were even more swollen from rubbing them and crying so profusely. My mother escorted me through the hospital and checked me in. The next thing I knew, we were in a super cold room.

I had no clue what was going on. All I wanted was to be healed of my back injury so I could play and to hold my girlfriend in my arms. I ran into the bathroom to call my girlfriend. She finally answered after twenty attempts.

"Please, please, please come see me," I begged. "I'm sorry Darryll, I can't," she said emotionless.

"What do you mean, you can't?! Why can't you!? Why won't you!? I'm in the hospital! I'm going to take my life! I need help! I need you! Why don't you care? Why won't you just come?" I yelled and pleaded.

"I just can't, Darryll. It wouldn't be right. I'm engaged now," she said.

It felt she was clawing at my heart with a dull knife every time she said that. We went back and forth and back and forth, but there was no convincing her to come see me. Just like sports, she was gone and never coming back. At some point I just hung up the phone and stormed out of the bathroom.

I came back to the hospital room even more hurt and angry.

The doctor walked into my room, introduced himself, and said, "So, tell me Darryll... why did you attempt to kill yourself?"

"I don't know ... I ... I ... I just don't want to live anymore," I mumbled while crying.

"Well, talk to me. What's been going on?" he asked gently.

"Leave me alone! I just want to die!" I responded holding my stomach and crying with anguish.

"No one here wants that, Da..."

"I don't care! Just let me die! I just want to die!" I said cutting him off.

The pain of trying to answer his questions was unbearable. I started crying uncontrollably.

The doctor exited the room to seek counsel and begin the process of admitting me to their psychiatric unit.

Then it happened.

A supernatural encounter

A female nurse with green pants walked into my room. She didn't introduce herself. She looked at my family and said, "He (referring to me) has no business being here." Then she turned toward me and spoke the words I'll never forget:

"I don't know who you are. And, I am not even supposed to be back here in this part of the hospital. But God told me to tell you that you need to say YES to Him," she said with gentle confidence.

"Yes, to Him?" I thought to myself.

In a matter of seconds my mind was flooded with a million thoughts. Who was this woman? What made her risk her job for me? God didn't say that to her. Not for me! I was a drug dealer, a womanizer, a thief, a pill addict and the furthest thing from religious. But why else would she risk her job if there wasn't some truth to what she was saying?

I concluded she was some crazy nurse and started crying again. Next thing I know this woman wrapped her arms around me and started praying for me. I can't remember a word she said because the longer she prayed, the harder I cried. Every word she spoke felt like a hammer trying to chisel through the stone-barrier I emotionally built around my heart. Her prayer felt like it took 30 seconds. My mother says it lasted almost five to 10 minutes. The nurse left and said she would come back to check on me in a few.

I wanted to die even more at that point. I was so angry at this woman and at "God." I had tried the religious thing as a child. My grandmother used to drag us all to church and make us sing in the choir. One day when I was 9 years old, the preacher asked if anyone wanted to put their faith in Jesus Christ. I stood up and walked to the front. I prayed what is known as the prayer of salvation. I got more involved in church. I joined a junior Deacons team, served as an usher, became more active in the choir and attended every event at the church. I prayed all the time and thought I had a relationship with God. A few of the pastors at the church started to mentor me. They let me stay at their house. They gave me life advice. They helped me learn how to serve in the church. This lasted for a few years.

Then the bottom of my "Christian" life started to fall out. One of the pastors who was mentoring me sold me a bunch of clothes that I thought were authentic brand names. Everyone laughed at me when I wore them to school because they were all fake. Another one of my pastor/mentors sexually molested a young girl in our church. Another pastor/mentor went to prison for a terrible crime he committed. Our church went from growing and exciting to declining and dramatic. Our lead pastor had a lot of his children serving in the church. His wife/their mother passed away. He later remarried, and his children hated it. Church became a place of family drama rather than a place to seek and serve God. All the drama and lack of character displayed in my pastors/mentors caused me to question my faith. Plus, being a Christian kept me from doing a lot of the fun stuff that other kids my age were doing. While they were going to parties and movies, I was at church conferences and prayer meetings.

I did a lot of research on faith, religion, secret societies and other realms of thought and came to the conclusion that religion was man-made foolishness. I concluded that the only reason I believed in Christianity in the first place was because I was born in America. I figured that if I were born in China, I would be a Buddhist. Or, if I were born in India, I would believe in Hinduism. I would essentially believe in whatever the predominate religion in a culture was. Originally, I thought all these religions led to the same God. Later, I developed a belief that all these religions were controlled by the Illuminati, Baphomet, members of the skull and bones fraternity or people from the Astro, Rockefeller or Rothschild bloodline.

The more I reflected on God, Jesus, religion, secret societies, my former sports life and former girlfriend, the angrier I got. Why was God so confusing? Why had I never heard about any of the secret societies until I did my own research? If God was real, why wouldn't He heal my back and allow me to play? Why does God allow so much evil to happen in this world? And, why did my girlfriend not want to be with me? Clearly, I thought, the problem was me. Something was wrong with me. I wasn't worthy of God's healing. I wasn't worthy of my ex-girlfriend's love. The only thing I had to offer the world was my athletic ability, and without that I was just another person sucking up air, working a boring 9-to-5 job that didn't compare to being an athlete. I was mad at the world. I hated God, and I hated myself.

I started to cry even harder as these thoughts raced through my mind. All of a sudden, my grandmother Greta burst through my hospital room door.

"Honey, I've been praying for you the entire way here. And God told me that you know exactly what to do. You need to say yes to Him!" she said huffing from shortness of breath.

My first thought was, "Yeah, yeah. Of course, my grandmother is supposed to say something religious." She was the one who always dragged us to church. Yet, I couldn't deny the ironic fact that she said the exact same thing the nurse with green pants said.

God wanted a yes from me.

But what would saying yes do? It wouldn't heal my back. It wouldn't bring back my girlfriend. It wouldn't change the world problems. It wouldn't erase all of the questions I had about faith. Saying yes seemed so pointless. I grew even more angry and started to cry uncontrollably again. My grandmother wrapped me in her arms and started praying. I remember feeling her warm hug and being torn between wanting to hug her back and wanting to push her away. She eventually stepped back. The heaviness in the room was so thick that the air around us felt like giant wet blankets. At this point, my dad, sister, and some of my other relatives were all packed in the room. Everyone was crying. No one knew what to do. We all just sat under the weight of my depression. But then something happened that completely shifted the atmosphere.

I heard the voice of God, as a still, small inner voice, say, "Son, will you just say yes to Me?" It was such a simple request, but it carried so much more meaning. I knew then that yes meant surrender and trust. God was asking me if I would surrender my doubts and trust in his goodness in spite of my depression, my pain, my doubts, my fears and my questions.

There was something about hearing God's voice that gave me the strength to mutter.

"Y..y..ee..ee..ee.ss.ss.s, God" in a sniffle-cry voice.
The moment I finished saying yes, the depression
I was struggling with immediately left the room. I
literally felt like 1,000 pounds had been lifted off of my
shoulders. It was the first time in months, maybe years,
that I felt so much hope. It felt so good, that I just kept
shouting, "Yes, Lord! Yes, Lord. Yes, Lord!"

The heavy blanket feeling switched to the feeling
of a light breeze on a sunny day, the more I yelled. My
swollen eyes were instantly healed, and I could open
them all the way. The joy I felt was indescribable. The
love I felt was unexplainable. The hope I had was irre-
placeable. Saying YES to God meant that I had put
my faith in Jesus Christ and His finished work on the
cross. It meant I was done trying to do life my way and
was fully surrendering to figuring out how to do life
Jesus' way. I knew in that moment my life had purpose
beyond sports if God, the Creator of the universe, the
Giver of life, chased after me when I wanted nothing
to do with Him. I knew He must see something in me
that I couldn't see in myself if He worked through two
women who didn't know each other just to get to me.

This was a catalytic moment that has been the driving force and most important aspect of loving my life
without sports. My relationship with Jesus has guided
me through these five phases of transition. It wasn't a
process I came up with myself. It was a process He took
me through to help me fall out of love with sports and
in love with Him and His plan for my life.

There have been many times when those suicidal
thoughts started to creep back into my mind. Every
time it happened, I would get the hope, strength and the
perspective I needed through prayer and His presence.
There were times when I was unsatisfied and unfulfilled
with life and my day job. That's when God would direct

me to a new path and give me the faith to take risks. It was Jesus Who helped me accept. Jesus Who helped me believe. Jesus Who helped me discover, pursue and persist. Without Him, I would be dead and missing out on the beautiful life I now get to experience.

Bad news

The bad news is there's not a person who has lived without telling a lie or thinking bad thoughts about someone. Many of us have done much worse. The Bible calls wrong things sin. We all have sinned and fallen short of God's standard of perfection (Romans 3:23).

The problem with our sin is that it separates us from God because He is completely perfect (holy) and cannot be in relationship with anyone who isn't perfect (holy). Not because He's mean, judgmental or complicated. But, because like oil and water, God and sin cannot mix.

The consequences of our sin are eternal separation from God (Romans 6:23).

Good news

The good news is that Jesus fixes all of this. Jesus was sent to Earth by God through the birthing of a virgin woman named Mary. This made Him fully man and fully God, so that He would represent humanity before God and God before humanity.

He lived perfectly for 33 years on earth and was crucified unjustly for sins He didn't commit so that He could save us from all the sins that we did and will commit.

It gets better.

Jesus didn't just die on the cross. He rose again and still lives (1 Corinthians 15:3-4)!

And the same spirit that raised Jesus from the dead is deposited into us when we put our faith in Him. It's His spirit that gives us assurance that when we die, we, too, will rise like He did to spend eternity with our Heavenly Father as we transition from this life to the next.

Not only do we get to spend eternity with our heavenly Father, but we get to abide with Him and experience the fullness of the life He desires for us now in this life.

"The thief does not come except to steal, and to kill, and to destroy. I have come that they may have life, and that they may have it more abundantly." (Jn 10:10 NKJV)

What must you do to be saved and experience this life?

All you have to do is believe.

"Jesus told them, "This is the only work God wants from you: Believe in the one he has sent." (Jn 6:29 NLT) "Because, if you confess with your mouth that Jesus is Lord and believe in your heart that God raised him from the dead, you will be saved." (Rom 10:9 ESV)

That's it. You can't earn salvation. Jesus earned it for you. You don't have to be a "good" person for God to love you. God already loves you.

To start a relationship with God, all you have to do is believe in Jesus by faith.

"For it is by grace you have been saved, through faith—and this is not from yourselves, it is the gift of God—not by works, so that no one can boast." (Eph 2:8-9 NIV)

Will you choose by faith to believe in Jesus today? Will you accept God's love for you? Will you say "yes" to His invitation like I did in the psychiatric unit?

God loves you just the way you are.

"But God showed his great love for us by sending Christ to die for us while we were still sinners." (Rom 5:8 NLT)

You don't have to wait until you "get your life together." You don't have to wait until you're in a church. I put my faith in Christ when I was high, depressed, agnostic and addicted to sex and drugs.

You can receive God's grace right now—just as you are, wherever you are.

Just say this prayer out loud.

Prayer of salvation

"Dear God. Thank You for Your love for me. I choose right now to put my faith in Jesus and His sacrifice for my sins. I pray that You guide me and help me to walk in the fullness of all that You have in store for me—from this day forward. In Jesus' name—Amen.

Did you say that prayer?

If you just said that prayer of salvation, congratulations! The Bible says that by putting your faith in the goodness of Jesus, you're now in right standing with God! (Rom 5:1) And all of Heaven is celebrating you right now! (Lk 15:7)

I want to celebrate with you, too, and help you get started growing in your relationship with the Lord. I have some free resources and advice I'd like to send to you. Visit secondchanceathletes.com/contact, or email connect@secondchanceathletes.com to share your story with us. I'm so excited for you! Your life after death is eternally secure, and your life in this world is forever changed. It's about to get real! It's going to be the most amazing journey ever.

Did you not say that prayer?

If you did not choose to say that prayer of salvation, Jesus and I still love you. I may not agree with your decision, but I respect you as a person. Let's stay connected. My team and I still want to be a blessing to you and help you live your best life after sports.

If you have any questions about faith, the transition out of athletics or life in general, feel free to email us or connect with us on social media. We're happy to help in any way we can.

You've got greatness inside you. It doesn't matter what you've been through or how many mistakes you've made. Always remember it's never too late to be great.

Life has a way of awarding us "second chances." And second chances exist so that we can finish strong. Finish strong, my friend.

—Darryll Stinson

NOTES

CHAPTER 1

1 *"Estimated Probability of Competing in College Athletics." NCAA online. April 8, 2020. http://www.ncaa.org/ about/resources/research/ estimated-probability-competing-college-athletics*

2 "NCAA Recruiting Facts: College sports create a pathway to opportunity for student-athletes." NCAA online. March, 2018. *https://www.ncaa.org/sites/ default/files/Recruiting%20Fact%20Sheet%20WEB.pdf*

3 Moreland-bishop, Leslie, "The Impact of Transition Out of Intercollegiate Athletics" (2009). All Dissertations. 397. *https://tigerprints.clemson.edu/ all_ dissertations/397*

4 *"Retired NFL Players Using Painkillers." Biomed Radio online. January 28, 2011. https://medicine.wustl.edu/ news/podcast/retired-nfl-players-using-painkillers/*

5   "Athletic Identity Impact on Sport Retirement and Career Transition Struggles for Collegiate Student-Athlete." UKDiss. com. June 6, 2019. *https://ukdiss.com/examples/ athletic-identity-impact-on-sport-retirement.php*

6   *Sharp, Andrew, "'Broke', and the Truth About Athletes and Money," SBNation (blog), October 3, 2012, https://www.sbnation.com/nfl/2012/10/3/3447168/ broke-espn-30-for-30-review*

7   *Reel, Justin J, Working Out: The Psychology of Sport and Exercise. California: Greenwood, 2015.*

CHAPTER 2

8   "Hater." Urban Dictionary. Accessed June 17, 2020. *https://www.urbandictionary.com/define. php?term=hater*

9   "Great Minds Discuss Ideas; Average Minds Discuss Events; Small Minds Discuss People." Quote Investigator. Accessed June 17, 2020. *https:// quote-investigator.com/2014/11/18/great-minds/*

CHAPTER 3

10   "Henry Thomas Buckle." Quote Investigator. Accessed June 17, 2020. *https://quoteinvestigator. com/tag/henry-thomas-buckle/*

11   Gregory, Christina. "The Five Stages of Grief: An Examination of the Kubler-Ross Model." Last modified April 11, 2019. *https://www.psycom.net/ depression.central.grief.html*

CHAPTER 5

12 "The Two Most Important Days in Your Life: The Day You Were Born and the Day You Discover Why." Quote Investigator. Accessed June 17, 2020. *https:// quoteinvestigator.com/2016/06/22/why/*

13 *http://www.brianpruitt.org/brian-pruitt*

CHAPTER 6

14 "Pursue." Merriam-Webster. Accessed June 17, 2020. *https://www.merriam-webster.com/dictionary/pursue*

15 *Nwoye, Tony, Getting Things Right: Laws of Proper Decision. Illinois: Revival Waves of Glory Books & Publishing, 2016.*

16 https://www.biography.com/actor/sylvester-stallone#:~:text=Early%20Life,Stallone%20had%20 a%20difficult%20childhood.

17 *Maxwell, John. Today Matters. New York: Warner Faith, 2004.*

18 Dornan, George. "There's a S.M.A.R.T. Way to Write Management's Goals and Objectives." AMA Forum, November, 1981. *https://community.mis. temple.edu/mis0855002fall2015/f iles/2015/10/ S.M.A.R.T-Way-Management-Review.pdf*

19 Hyatt, Michael. "The Beginner's Guide to Goal Setting: Five Goal-Setting Principles for Getting Bigger, Better Results." Michael Hyatt & Co. (blog), Last modified June 14, 2013. *https://michaelhyatt. com/goal-setting/*

20 *Covey, Stephen R.. The 7 Habits of Highly Effective People. United States: Mango Media, 2015.*

21 *"Boojie." Dictionary.com. Accessed June 1, 2020. https:// www.dictionary.com/browse/boojie*

CHAPTER 7

22 Newland, Stephen. "The Power of Accountability." Last modified 2018. *https://www.afcpe.org/ news-and-publications/the-standard/2018-3/ the-power-of-accountability/*

23 "Five Reasons You Should Budget."Turbotax (blog), June 3, 2010, *https://blog.turbotax.intuit.com/tax-tips/ five-reasons-you-should-budget-3264/*

24 "80% of Americans Have This But Don't Want It." Dave Ramsey (blog), 2020, *https://www.daveramsey. com/blog/americans-have-debt*

25 *"New to Budgeting? Why You Should Try the 50-20-30 Rule." Forbes.com, June 11, 2016. https://www.forbes.com/sites/trulia/2016/07/11/ new-to-budgeting-why-you-should-try- the-50-20-30-rule/#459fc24632e9*

26 Dudley, Chris. "Money Lessons Learned from Pro Athletes' Financial Fouls." CNBC online. Last modified May 15, 2018. *https://www.cnbc.com/2018/05/14/ money-lessons-learned-from-pro-athletes-financial-fouls. html#:~:text=At%20last%20look%2C%20an%20 estimated,just%20two%20years%20after%20retirement.*

27 *Preston, Chris. "Five Reasons Professional Athletes Go Broke." Wyatt Investment Research (blog), March 25, 2013,* https://www.wyattresearch.com/article/ five-reasons-professional-athletes-go-broke/#:~: -text=Major%20League%20Baseball%20(MLB)%20 players,from%201.36%20million%20in%202011.

28 Crooks, Ross. "From Stoked to Broke: Why Are So Many Professional Athletes Going Bankrupt?" Intuit Mint Life (blog), February 22, 2013, *https://blog.mint.com/how-to/f rom-stoked- to-broke-why-are-so-many-professional-athletes -going-bankrupt-0213/?display=wide*

29 "Research Statistic on Financial Windfalls and Bankruptcy." National Endowment for Financial Education, January 2018. *https://www.nefe.org/press-room/ news/2018/research-statistic-on-financial-windfalls- and-bankruptcy.aspx#:~:text=DENVER%20 %E2%80%94%20Over%20the%20past%20couple, receiving%20a%20large%20financial%20windfall.*

30 "Mary Anne Radmacher Quotes." Goodreads.com. Accessed May 25, 2020. *https://www.goodreads.com/ author/quotes/149829.Mary_Anne_Radmacher*

31 "Proverbs 24:16" Biblehub.com. Access May 25, 2020. *https://biblehub.com/proverbs/24-16.htm*

32 Darryll Stinson. We All Need Hope. December 28, 2019. *https://www.youtube.com/watch?v= L1IwC0RiC58*

33 "Christine Caine Quotes." Goodreads.com. Accessed May 25, 2020. *https://www.goodreads. com/quotes/7072229-sometimes-when-you-r e-in-a-dark-place-you-think-you-ve*

34 "N.R. Walker Quotes." Goodreads.com. Accessed May 25, 2020. *https://www.goodreads.com/quote s/9830915-whenever-you-find-yourself-doubtin g-how-far-you-can-go*

35 "Sometimes it takes an overwhelming breakdown to have an undeniable breakthrough." Consciousmagazine. co. Accessed May 25, 2020. *https://consciousmagazine. co/sometimes-it-takes-an-overwhelming-breakdow n-to-have-an-undeniable-breakthrough/*

36 "Our deepest fear is not that we are inadequate. Our deepest fear is that we are powerful beyond measure." Quotes investigator. Accessed May 25, 2020. *https:// quoteinvestigator.com/2019/06/30/deepest/*

37 "If You Can't Fly, Then Run." Literary Devices. Accessed May 1, 2020. *https://literarydevices.net/ if-you-cant-fly-then-run/*

Made in United States
North Haven, CT
05 February 2024

48293637R00104